(Continued from front flap)

resources are available for this and the Green Revolution but they are "presently used for other purposes, such as maintaining nuclear arsenals, puppet states, and counter-insurgency wars." The book concludes that "the great clamor of exhaustion being raised... is but the wail of a sluggish social system." A tough polemic for "the other side" of the zero-growth question, universally recommended.

ROBERT KATZ is the author of *Death in Rome, Black Sabbath,* and *The Fall of the House of Savoy*. The Chicago Tribune called *Death in Rome* "a masterpiece of literature–a masterpiece of historical scholarship." It is now being made into a film by Carlo Ponti starring Richard Burton and Marcello Mastroianni.

Mr. Katz has worked for the United Nations and has been a consultant to the international development review CERES. A specialist in social history, he is a Fellow of the John Simon Guggenheim Foundation and a grantee of the American Council of Learned Societies.

Jacket design by Tim Gaydos

A GIANT IN THE EARTH

ALSO BY ROBERT KATZ

Death in Rome
Black Sabbath
The Fall of the House of Savoy

A GIANT IN THE EARTH

by

ROBERT KATZ

STEIN AND DAY / ***Publishers*** / **New York**

First published in 1973

Library of Congress Catalog Card No. 72-83222

Published simultaneously in Canada by Saunders of Toronto, Ltd.
Designed by Bernard Schleifer
Printed in the United States of America
Stein and Day/*Publishers*/7 East 48 Street, New York, N.Y. 10017
ISBN 0-8128-1521-1

TO
Oscar Ochs

CONTENTS

AUTHOR'S NOTE

THIS IS AN essay on some of the social implications of the "green revolution." Until now the green revolution has been a relatively quiet phenomenon, though not always peaceful. Fundamentally it is a technological revolution rather than ideological, agricultural rather than political, but it is as portentous and as forceful as any upheaval can be.

It is new. It is big—perhaps, as some say, it may turn out to be the biggest event of the century. It started small a few years ago, developed and tried by a handful of men. But rather startling results, uniqueness, unusual circumstance, and irresistible pressures have allowed it to proceed somewhat spectacularly throughout many parts of the underdeveloped world, and have given it meaning for people in all countries both rich and poor.

Like all revolutions of substance, the green revolution adumbrates new times and new, radical ideas. It augurs well and threatens. By its own internal logic it belies much of what the world of the 1960s came to believe about hunger, population growth, and the Malthusian nightmare in which famine, poverty, and misery are thought to be a natural condition of man. It threatens to upset thoroughly the world balance of power, bringing on all the political, economic, and social consequences implied. It also threatens, if it is not carefully guarded, ecological disturbances of unheard-of, almost universal proportions, which would dwarf current environmental and urban problems. On the other hand, it carries an elusive promise of a more rational, humane, and less troubled world.

The reader should know that I am not a specialist in any of the disciplines upon which the green revolution is having its greatest impact. I am not an agronomist, biologist, chemist, demographer, ecologist, economist, geneticist, nor sociologist, although I have relied heavily on the work of these specialists. I usually study and write about modern social history. A couple of years ago, while engaged in this activity, I was asked to serve as a consultant to an international review concerned with the problems of economic and social development in the world's underdeveloped countries. My contribution to this somewhat unusual journal was quite modest, but I had had placed at my disposal a sizable amount of documentary and analytical literature on the subject, much of it unpublished, and a large portion of it dealing with the burgeoning green revolution.

What struck me was that here was an entirely new historical development, apparently of vast potential, which simply did not square with the neo-Malthusian interpretation of past and contemporary history, an interpretation which in the late 1960s was achieving a very wide consensus, particularly in the United States and all the wealthy nations. In other words, what Malthus had said in 1798—that population will invariably expand beyond the means of subsistence and that therefore hunger, famine, disease, misery, and vice must necessarily accompany mankind to eternity—and what the neo-Malthusians had elaborated in a popular conception that viewed the population "explosion" more or less as the world's greatest evil—was being seriously undermined by the progress of the green revolution. The inherent powers of the new technology gave it a capability of providing a primary life support—food—for an astronomic number of people, while population could only grow, regardless of the rate, to whatever might be the maximum number imposed by the space limitations of this planet. When calculated, the latter number is seen to be infinitely less than the former.

Food production, however, though the neo-Malthusians make much of its supposedly restricted nature, is only one aspect of man's relationship to his environment, which consists of such components as ecological balance, resource use, and above all the distribution and application of social power—a major variable often more neglected than the first two. But the surprising ability of the green revolution to outrun the unprecedented high-speed population growth we are witnessing seemed to me in 1969 to be worthy of further investigation, especially since it stood in direct contradiction to the life-negating pessimism—not to mention activities—one heard then and still hears today.

My decision to proceed with the necessary research, which was favored by privileged access to essential materials and an opportunity to travel to some of the areas where the effects of the green revolution are most profound, led to this book. It also led me to the conclusion that while there is much cause for pessimism, there are signs of much hope, and few of the neo-Malthusian prophecies are inevitable. Further, it appears that the entire conception is useful to only a very small segment of society—those who benefit most from the preservation or enhancement of the status quo—and in many of its aspects it may be harmful to almost everyone else.

It is generally unwise to write a book on a subject containing elements concerning which the author lacks the expertise of those highly trained in such fields. I know that I am treading on dangerous ground. Sometimes, however, in this case for reasons I hope will be made plain by what follows, it seems appropriate to raise doubts about some of the views held by the experts, in spite of the undeniable risks incurred. I have no pretensions about having explored at great depth any of the topics discussed herein, nor about having produced a disciplined, scientific study. That much at least is always best left to the experts. My own research is documented in the "Notes" section of this book, and I have endeavored to adhere to the known rather than the supposed, but my purpose has been to probe not to prove; I have sought not answers but questions.

ROBERT KATZ

Rome, June, 1972

MR. GODWIN[1]

The spirit of oppression, the spirit of servility, and the spirit of fraud, these are the immediate growth of the established administration of property. They are alike hostile to intellectual [and moral] improvement. The other vices of envy, malice, and revenge are their inseparable companions. In a state of society where men lived in the midst of plenty, and where all shared alike the bounties of nature, these sentiments would inevitably expire. The narrow principle of selfishness would vanish. No man being obliged to guard his little store, or provide with anxiety and pain for his restless wants, each would lose his individual existence in the thought of the general good. No man would be an enemy to his neighbours, for they would have no subject of contention, and of consequence philanthropy would resume the empire which reason assigns her. Mind would be delivered from her perpetual anxiety about corporal support, and be free to expatiate in the field of thought which is congenial to her. Each would assist the inquiries of all.

MR. MALTHUS

Man cannot live in the midst of plenty. All cannot share alike the bounties of nature. Were there no established administration of property, every man would be obliged to guard with force his little store. Selfishness would be triumphant. The subjects of contention would be perpetual. Every individual would be under a constant anxiety about corporal support, and not a single intellect would be left free to expatiate in the field of thought.

How little Mr. Godwin has turned his attention to the real state of human society will sufficiently appear from the manner in which he endeavours to remove the difficulty of a super abundant population.

MR. GODWIN

The obvious answer to this objection is that to reason thus is to foresee difficulties at a great distance. Three-fourths of the habitable globe are now uncultivated. The parts already cultivated are capable of immeasurable improvement. Myriads of centuries of still increasing population may pass away, and the earth be still found sufficient for the subsistence of its inhabitants.

MR. MALTHUS

No reason can be assigned why, under the circumstances supposed, population should not increase faster than in any known instance. If then we were to take the period of doubling at fifteen years . . . and reflect upon the labour necessary to double the produce in so short a time, even if we allow it possible, we may venture to pronounce with certainty that, if Mr. Godwin's system of society were established, instead of myriads of centuries, not thirty years could elapse before its utter destruction from the simple principle of population.

A GIANT IN THE EARTH

PROLOGUE

With the development of agriculture and the rise of neolithic society, perhaps 10,000 years ago, the human race gradually came to settlement with the heroic beast nature used to be. Then, for an age never known before or afterward, man, in almost all his frail numbers, lived at peace with his gods, his neighbors, and the vexatiousness of his body and soul.

Man had come down from the trees and had wandered through the blood-soaked forests for half a million years. With the sword of his sexuality and the multitude of powers inherent in his agile hands, he had outwitted all other living things, all the shifting of the winds, and fires in the sky. But he had studied the ruthless way, emerging as a predator, and the only thing he really knew well, despite romantic tales we hear today, was how to strike a stunning blow and kill.

The conquests of the primal hunter were of the most unenduring kind; they had to be renewed with the dawn of every day. He could fell a tree, or tear a fruit from its highest branch, but he had no knowledge of the gentle secret of coaxing plentitude from plants. He could slay an animal far more powerful than he, and feast for a day or two; but he did not know how to make the living animal serve him for ten or twenty years. He had few friends among the creatures with whom he lived, but his enemies were manifold, and sometimes they were of his own kind. Thus he lived in darkness and in fear, and we know from the melancholy paintings on his caves that he starved for love.

He was a hungry, sorry manner of a man. Though proficient and wise in ways that must still be relearned, he could find no rest for his weary bones, driven endlessly from wood to wood by the capriciousness of fortune and an economy that precluded the possibility of settling down. Time and the infinite trail that had to be smoothed had bequeathed him restless genes and a troubled soul, and we can still hear his whimper (as well as our own) in his three most permanent creations: language, the arts, and the gods. This paleolithic hunter may be said to be our paternal ancestor. His opposite number, whom he first raped, then married in a most holy way, was the flower of the New Stone Age. She and the hunter made history.

Probably it was a woman, sitting observantly among wild plants and chewing the gut of a freshly slain beast for its thread, who discovered agriculture. In any event, neolithic society, signaled by that covenant with nature that promised respite from the hunt, and food and love as the wages of a nurtured soil, was the glory of womankind. Lewis Mumford, who has often written on this score, has seen the connection between plowing the soil and the surge of sexual desire settled woman gave to man. Both of these activities—resulting in a surplus food supply and a greatly expanded population—were essential preconditions for the transition from being anchored in the mud to a life that knows the sun and has gone to meet the stars.

With the beginning of cultivation, says Mumford, "women's sexual characteristics become symbolically significant: the menstrual onset of puberty, the breaking of the hymen, the penetration of the vulva, the milking of her breasts, make her own life a model for the rest of creation." [1] It was neolithic woman, he has written, who wielded the digging stick or hoe: "she who tended the garden crops and accomplished those masterpieces of selection and cross-fertilization which turned raw wild species into the prolific and richly nutritious domestic varieties: it was woman who made the first containers, weaving baskets and coiling the first clay pots. In form, the village, too, is her creation: for whatever else the village might be, it was a collective nest for the care and nurture of the young."

The first bowl was modeled on Aphrodite's breast, and the greatest container of them all was and remains ever-fertile, always pregnant Mother Earth.

The practice of agriculture and animal husbandry—the taming at long last of man, beast, and flower—ushered in that singular epoch of security, peace, and stability. Neolithic society was an unfamiliar era of cooperation, of the communal sharing of man's goods, and of a rounding of the individual, who knew neither masters nor slaves. His chattels were meager, but his estates were without frontier. There was little craving for power in the village, and war in the neolithic world was probably unthought of and, in any case, impossible. He had no wicked past to climb upon his back and weigh him down. He created morality and virtue. His future was known. In exchange for a promise to return after use all that he needed or fancied, nature issued her bounty, pouring it forth with a generosity that assured his existence for as long as the sun might shine.

The fulfillment of this obligation required discipline, order, prudence, repetitiousness, permanence, unchanging routine, and all the other qualities demanded of earthbound, peasant man. It meant forgoing the beckoning path, subduing the urge to possess, and postponing the call of desire. Gone, or rather contained at great effort in the soul of man, were Vico's poetic "giants," those first men who owed their size to the wild and strenuous life in the wood, who copulated shamelessly in the sight of heaven, and sang before they invented speech. Now, says Vico, they had learned "to check their bestial habit of wandering wild through the great forest of the earth, and acquired the contrary custom of remaining . . . settled in their fields. Hence they later became the founders of the nations . . ." [2]

Thus the singing hunters grew short and stocky, and without doubt phlegmatic. They were passive now, cautious, punctual, and introspective—easy pickings for the last remaining heroes. For the bells of the new village had tolled an end to the hunt, but not to all the hunters. Paleolithic men, perhaps the fittest of their breed, still survived. Miscast for the new times, they were endowed with an adventurous heart, which could not support the regular beat of peasant life. Yet the chase had lost its flavor; few men hunt when food and drink abounds. The old pleasures of the kill could hardly be awakened. A fence was more efficient than a spear. The skills taught in the forest were scarcely needed now. The diehards of the oldest, longest age were all but unemployed, and their antiquated weapons were falling into disuse.

Unable to give up a calling that even today still rings in man's soul, they lived in lawless gangs, practicing their archaic arts, but preying, too, when inevitable hungers panged, on the affluent, defenseless new society, whose churlish ways they surely did despise. The hunter became the aboriginal bandit. He stole the pearls of wheat calloused hands had gathered. He guzzled the wine and beer the patient people had learned to brew. He seized wealth from all their labors; then he dragged their women to his stronghold, adding violence to his crimes. Such was the way men began to make history.

Two hundred generations ago the orgy that gave birth to civilization was more or less complete. The horde of primeval gangsters had come out of the forest for the last time, led by the fathers of Gilgamesh and the hunter Enkidu, who was made of mud and grew up among the wild beasts. Their loins girded with lion skins, they rode hard on the peasants and stayed. They built a wall around the village, and announced themselves as the lords of the law and the land, sent not from the niggardly woods, but from the kingdom of the gods.

Human blood flowed at the union of decadent paleolithic culture to the static, self-satisfied New Stone Age. It was the liquid with which the first priests baptized modern times. These were events attended by the gods, for the gods were now captive of the hunter-kings, taken into everlasting bondage. They exalted the new unity, which had been determined by the discovery of the greatest, most consequential truth yet known to men: that the cleaving of their kind into haves and have-nots, the division of their labors into artless, stupefying bits, and the rule by the strong over the weak were the ways to release that dimensionless, inexhaustible power with which oppressed, historic man began, and continues to this day, his blind conquest of heaven and earth.

Thus the advent of agriculture and an increased population, the combination of which allowed production of a surplus of food and other goods, had permitted the vanishing hunters to abandon their traditional pursuits. Turning the weapons of the forest against ill-protected, settled man, they established themselves as the first ruling elite, the new class of lords deft at defending its self-proclaimed nobility by cracking the challenger's skull.

Putting mankind asunder and accumulating wealth from the labors of others, however, taught the lesson that the new social order was fragile and required lasting reinforcement. Of such needs the laws and records were made, and writing was given its day. Lines were drawn on properties, which now grew as hard to come by as they were untouchable by all who had none.

Through the agency of the supernatural, venerated hunters fathered kings, and kings created armies, and armies, requiring, like their lords and their kings, ever-greater quantities of surpluses and wealth from toiling people, created war. War, and the subjugation of the weaker social enclaves by the mightier, permitted increasingly larger unities, and unities gave rise to nations.

By continual war, by the growth and discipline of working populations, and by the commerce of science, capital, and goods on terms regulated by the distribution of social power, the wealth of nations increased, and increases. But a chronic irony of historic times thus far has been that mankind grows faster than the store of his goods, that there is never enough wealth to go around.

As the fortunes of some nations went well, the poverty of others was not then redressed, and, as everyone knows, in even the rich nations the poor continue to live. The cloven system of haves and have-nots is still with us, causing avarice, envy, and meanness. The hunters remain at the helm. Blood is let every day.

For fifty centuries we have lived this way, and the permanence of human anguish and injustice, in spite of beauty, revolutions, and some goodness, has led many to believe that it must always be so. Hopes and plans for an abundance that might free mankind from all that divides and degrades him are rejected. Brotherhood is scoffed at. The approach of a filthy end, in which a sickening, impoverished mass of men will totally foul the earth, is the first vision of our day. The intimidated and the uneasy affluent see the strict limitation of life and the expansion of death as among man's noblest goals. In many cases they have unfairly won our support and confidence. But as they cannot discover how to relieve the suffering many, they have grown to desire the elimination not of the suffering but of the many.

It seems an odd paradox, however, that such a mighty cry for scaling down both our aspirations and our very existence as a species, which owes all its past successes to its differentiated multiplication, can be heard so loudly at this particular point in history. It is hardly fashionable to say so, but it is strange indeed, as Malcolm Muggeridge has observed, that the alarm has come "precisely when the possibilities in the way of food production are seen to be virtually illimitable, and when the whole universe is about to be opened up, providing space to accommodate a million, million times our present squalid little family." [3]

The grace and wherewithal of nature are far from strained. This planet alone can well provide for at least 100 billion of our kind—many times more than our present 3.5 billion. The great clamor of exhaustion being raised at the mere doorstep of the larger figure is but the wail of a sluggish social system unable to expel the giant now stirring in the earth. It is the stark confession of historic society's massive failure to command the powers of its own creation. That it whines loudest in our time is because ours is the time in which all doubt has been dispelled that man is a creature of meager means. The discovery of nuclear energy, the journey to the moon, and the present agricultural renaissance called the "green revolution" are the good tidings announcing the possibility, if not the coming, of tetherless, posthistoric man.

To be sure, the news has not been received quite this way, and it is hard to be sanguine before all manner of continued hunger, disease, and war. But man's potential is not decreased by the failure of one or another generation to understand it.

Today the long-established hunter elites, their self-sanctified institutions, and all who have gained or pursue their favors are being challenged by swiftly growing numbers of people. Their appearance on earth in the age of affluence raises the level of their demands to no less than the well-being of all. The sorry tale of the universal dearth no longer rings true. Oppressive rule is at last creating the very means by which it no longer need endure. But the rulers themselves are a tenacious breed, often more concerned with their hold on power than with the use of that power itself.

Thus the challenge entails clash and struggle, and there is not the slightest assurance that the continuum of history—the rule of the hunters—will not prevail for still another unknowable number of years.

There is a giant in the earth, but there is as yet no satisfying way to set him free.

I

FLOWER POWER

THE POETRY OF the first people is still in us, for it takes no great literary eye to perceive that wheat is like a penis. That the plant has a shaft, a sheath, and a head; that it is worthless when it falls, and stands tallest and most florid at the moment it yields the pearly seed of its future generations led to a colossal, universal misjudgment, which remained for the green revolution to overthrow.

The orgy-loving goddess Demeter gave us the gift of wheat, and all the other high-standing cereals such as corn, rice, and rye, but it was men and women who raised them, observed them, and tended their many breeds. It could only have been a powerful inclination that made man favor, and so select and multiply for thousands of years, those cereals that stood highest in the field. Mind and reason would have sought the stubby, short-stemmed plant, which showed defiance to the winds that sweep the plain and the burdens of the rains.

Tall was beautiful, however, and when the vicissitudes of weather often made the towering stalk droop and fall

all but lifeless on its stocky, less attractive neighbors, its failure was lamented; yet the virtues of smallness somehow remained unseen.

By the twentieth century, men had long ago forgotten the old songs, but the size of a man's grain was still being celebrated in the countryside and in the city's music halls. In the midwestern United States proud farmers crowed, "*Iowa, Iowa, that's where the tall corn grows,*" while the Broadway stage taught all America to sing about the corn high as a elephant's eye, climbing clear up to the sky.

So were men's wishful thoughts expressed not very long ago. But the green revolution is the time of the hard-nosed dwarf.

When, in the fall of 1970, the Nobel prize for peace was given to an Iowa farmer named Norman Borlaug for "fathering" the green revolution, relatively few people had ever heard of his work, much less of the man. The green revolution, an anonymous journalist's catch-phrase now hammered by lead into an embarrassing cliché, remained unannounced until 1968. It had started quite modestly a few years before (although Borlaug's role dates to 1944) in the middle of a decade that had early grown unaccustomed to any semblance of good news.

The ten-year frame in which the green revolution quietly gained momentum was the turn of Cuban nuclear roulette, assassination, and the nauseating count of lifeless bodies. The callous dwarf was driving out the tall grains, but the word was of the coming silent springtime and the fact that mother's milk was getting foul; lights burned low, poverty went out of hiding, a wave of human feces came home from the sea, the "population bomb" was found, and "the famines" were on the way. Small wonder the green revolution had no fame.

As early as 1964 Borlaug, speaking of his work to a rather obscure agricultural scientific society, was saying that now "man can feed the world's mushrooming human population for the next 100 to 200 years."[1] This was before the green revolution had proved itself on the scale with which it is sweeping through much of the underdeveloped world today. But even Borlaug was to lose faith in his own words. In the sixties the doomsayers were having their day.

The twice-cursed failure of the monsoon on the Indian subcontinent in 1965 and 1966, to which the United States responded by feeding 60 million Indians for two years, gave license, credibility, and unequal time to only one school of thought. When the noted French agronomist René Dumont declared in 1967 that he had been authorized by the United Nations Food and Agriculture Organization (FAO) to state that mankind was on the threshold of famine, he was only rushing forward to update his famous prediction that "The world will face the greatest famine in history by about 1980."[2] The Paddock brothers, who advocated that the United States write off India, Egypt, and about half the world in all as "can't-be-saved" countries, which should be negatively aided along the road to oblivion, refashioned their 1964 book *Hungry Nations* and called it *Famine—1975!*[3] And Paul Ehrlich in 1968 gave us *The Population Bomb,* in which he proclaimed on his first page:

> The battle to feed all of humanity is over. In the 1970s the world will undergo famines—hundreds of millions of people are going to starve to death. At this late date nothing can prevent [this] . . . We [Americans] are today involved in the events leading to famine; tomorrow we [Americans] may be destroyed by its consequences. . . . Population control is the only answer.[4]

The growth in numbers of human beings was a "cancer," said the book (my copy of which comes from its nineteenth printing in two years); "the cancer itself must be cut out"; "by compulsion if voluntary methods fail." [5]

After all this, Borlaug apparently felt constrained to come down from his higher estimations. By 1970 he had made a descent of more than an entire century. Replying to the Nobel committee's generous statement that he had made possible the elimination of hunger, the American said that in fact "We have only delayed the world food crisis for another thirty years" [6] (he has subsequently reduced this to twenty). He was reminded that when the dwarf wheat strain was first introduced into Pakistan, a rumor spread swiftly among the peasants that it would make all the women who ate it sterile. "If only that were true," he said quite unguardedly, "we would really merit the Nobel Peace Prize." [7]

Whether or not the modest Dr. Borlaug is a worthy laureate is something best left for the prize-givers to ponder, should anyone care to. Whether, however, the man's contribution to the dramatic advances now taking place in agriculture—as a component of the technological revolution in general—forces us to completely rethink in the 1970s the grim, powerful, pernicious, and enduring ideas laid down in the 1960s we shall consider here.

People began to take notice of the ugly dwarf when in some places high-standing wheat could no longer perform. This happened first, on a significant scale, in Japan. It coincides with the qualitative escalation in the pre-World War II use of fertilizers, an arcane technology recommended by Moses, practiced by Odysseus' father, but one whose time did not really come until a score of years ago.

In the 1870s, shortly after the fall of the shoguns, the Japanese began to feel more crowded than ever before. The first effect of this sentiment familiar to many nations has always been the intensification of agriculture, and in Japan, with its scarcity of soils, alleviation of the feeling required an increase in the use of fertilizer. Now, however, the traditional solution failed. The tallest wheats grew taller still; their stalks thinned until at last, top-heavy with seed, they collapsed. Fortunately a native short-strawed variety existed, a wheat the Japanese called *Daruma,* named for a squat little doll that rocks at the slightest touch but always comes to rest in a standing position.[8] The ancestry of this plant remains unknown, but it represented the surviving line of a mutant, a single kernel of wheat that had been rendered strange by the sun and husbanded by at least one man who valued poetic oddity over poetic size. Today controlled plant mutation is an established feature of the green revolution.

The Japanese mated Daruma with an American variety named *Fultz,* and their small offspring was crossed with another American, a certain *Turkey Red.* Judging from the results, it was a happy union, which produced a singular breed of dwarfs with a unique proclivity for taking up large amounts of fertilizer and converting it not into shaft but into head. This species of wheat, named *Norin,* helped keep the Japanese, if not their ill-won empire, well fed, but here the matter rested, unobserved by the outside world until Japan lost World War II.

The dwarfs were seen by the conquerors in the person of S. C. Salmon, an American agricultural scientist, who literally could not believe his eyes. They had been planted, he took note, "on land that had been heavily fertilized and irrigated. In spite of these very favorable conditions for vegetative growth the plants were [only] about twenty-four inches high, but stood erect. They produced so many stems and there were so many heads, a second look was necessary to verify the fact that the rows were twenty inches apart instead of the common six to ten inches in the United States."[9]

Salmon took the more-than-half-American plant home.

A wheat-breeder named Orville A. Vogel began now to experiment with the dwarfs in the soils of the Pacific Northwest. They behaved poorly away from Japan. They mated promiscuously with neighboring plants, were prone to contract diseases, and generally grew up wrong. But Vogel persevered. He tamed them until they were properly bred, teaching them to act well in their adopted land; then, when they were impeccably finished, he crossed them with an all-American wheat, and he called their progeny *Gaines.*

Gaines wheat was a celebrated champion, which set world-record yields in its day, but the Nobel committee gave the peace prize to Borlaug, not his forerunners—and for just reason. Hitherto, as Lester Brown has pointed out, nearly all the important developments in agricultural technology had been made in, and for the benefit of, the favored nations of the temperate zones. Brown writes in terms perhaps a bit too forgiving:

> Even though a great deal of research has been devoted to plantation agriculture in the tropics, the prime beneficiaries have been outsiders, those in the rich countries to whom the commodities are sold. Those in the tropics were at best residual beneficiaries, forced to make do with an agricultural technology developed in northwestern Europe, the United States, or Japan, a technology admirably adapted to the temperate climates but usually poorly suited to the tropics.[10]

While the tropics were being forced to "make do" with the white man's technology, white technologists were disdaining the low agricultural productivity of the tropics. This "hopeless" condition, it was often said or implied, was the fault of the laziness of Mexicans, the dishonesty of Indians, and the black belt of ignorance girding the planet between the Tropics of Cancer and Capricorn. The green revolution, on the other hand, which bares these notions for what they are, represents the widespread application of the first technology aimed at exploiting the leverage tropical climates have on the temperate.

Such was Borlaug's achievement. A plant scientist who had begun his career with Du Pont, he had been sent to Mexico in 1944 by the Rockefeller Foundation with vague instructions "to help Mexico help herself." [11] The story of how he carried out his mandate forms the background of the green revolution, but it is also a reenactment of an older, more familiar tale about how the rich often get richer.

When thirty-year-old Borlaug arrived in Mexico City to join three of his foundation colleagues, who had been dispatched there the year before, it could hardly have been foreseen in New York that his Rockefeller-funded philanthropic work would result in a revolution not only in agriculture but particularly in the use of chemical fertilizer. Modern fertilizer production, which has tripled in the past twenty years and is expected to catapult five times present output by 1985, is a petroleum-based industry, one in which the Rockefellers have a commercial interest. But this is our way of progress, and should be gainsaid only with caution. It ought also to be borne in mind that if nonprofit research is often later spun into gold, gold many times, too, unravels into new knowledge through the agents of science, for whom it pays.

A Giant in the Earth

What Borlaug did in the first two decades of his tenure was to mate 60,000 different species of wheat, and in forty plant generations create the all-tropical race of dwarfs and "double-" and "triple-dwarfs," which has so transformed the outlook for the future of the world.

In 1964 Borlaug went before the annual meeting of the American Phytopathological Society and described his accomplishment as "fantastic." [12]

To an audience of scientists, many of whom were firmly convinced of the imminence of "the worst famine in history," as one of them phrased it, he began almost brazenly:

> The views that I present may be very different from those many of you hold. Your views are largely conditioned by the scientific roles your researches have played in the agriculture of the outstanding food-surplus area of the world, whereas mine are based upon twenty years . . . in food-deficient countries.[13]

Not since Sigmund Freud affirmed his theory of infantile sexuality had a scientist come forward before his peers so boldly. Borlaug stated that on the basis of his experiments, "I see no technical reason why the yield and national production of wheat in both India and Pakistan [then facing severe food shortages] cannot be doubled within eight years and tripled within twelve years." Indeed, he went further, they could even be quadrupled in a decade, and not only on the Asian subcontinent but in the Near and Middle East, too. This was to launch him in the pre-Nobel-prize period that followed into a series of "wild" predictions, all of which have, with months and even years to spare, come true.

In his wide-ranging 1964 speech he spoke of a future

that an ecologically alarmed present refuses to recognize. The world's agricultural land, he noted, could be expanded by a multiple of five. Few people are aware of "the tremendous food production potential" of the underdeveloped world, he said. He foresaw a connection between space research and food production on earth. Any life-support system developed for deep-space travel, he said, would require waste recycling, and this would have implications for future processes of this kind on a planetary scale. Finally, he understood that the inevitable solution to the mystery of photosynthesis "would make today's agriculture largely obsolete and make food production a branch of the chemical industry." This went one stage further than Godwin, who had once predicted that man would one day grow his entire food supply in a single flowerpot.

Few people heard Borlaug's address. Fewer still remember it today. But his strange nation of dwarfs has multiplied beyond even his expectations, and his forecast that "what is true of wheat is almost certain to be true also for many other food crops" has come to be.

All this was patterned after Borlaug's genetic masterpiece. The first thing he did "to help Mexico help herself" (and in the process create the new technology) was to breed a variety of wheat that could resist its traditional enemy, a plant disease called "rust." Mexican wheats, whose ancestors had arrived in that country accidentally mixed into a bag of rice carried there by Cortes, were particularly debilitated. They were prone to rust, a fungus that emaciates the plant and tarnishes stem and leaves with powdery spores the color of iron left out in the rain.

Conquering rust was an exercise that took thirteen years, and while it was being performed, Borlaug was programming the plant generations to pass on three additional traits. One of these came about by inlaying precious genes that rendered the plant indifferent to the variations of tropical climates and soils. Its value would be seen in the high adaptability of the plant, which was made to feel at home anywhere on the globe within a latitude of some 5,000 miles, instead of the 500-mile range within which temperate-zone wheats could thrive.

A second encoding in the new plant's DNA was aimed at making the entire organism aloof to the time of year and the length of day. The wheat of the temperate-zone man, like the man himself, had been conditioned to work by the temperate-zone clock. Wheat was sown in the darkness of winter, and when the days grew longer, the plant "knew" that its flowering time had come. In the tropics, descending toward the equator, winter disappears and night and day grow equal all the year around. This is most upsetting to plants native to the north. They take on the very attributes of slothfulness and feebleness so carelessly ascribed to their hosts.

Borlaug bred his race insensitive to the itineraries of light. His sophisticated plant rose above all manner of seasons, as unmoved by the comings and goings of the equinoxes as it was inured to the period in which it was asked to perform. While conventional plants, like old-time sailors, went forward by taking readings of the northern sky, the new wheat ran on built-in tropical time.

This was a radical innovation. It allowed for the efficient use of the abounding excess of solar energy that the tropics have over all the other circles on the globe, a valuable gift of nature hitherto squandered recklessly.

Thus the color-blind plant matured in a certain number of days in any set of months, and this meant that in the tropics, not one but two crops of wheat could be grown in a single year. A green revolution was in the air.

The finishing touch came when Borlaug hitched Vogel's champion Gaines dwarf to his own creation. Eight years later he had superwheat, a plant, when double-cropped, capable of yielding twenty times as much edible grain as the national average had been when Borlaug first came to Mexico. Mexico went rapidly from a nation that had to import half its wheat needs every year, to self-sufficiency, and on to becoming a wheat exporter.

Pint-sized superwheat proved to be a most remarkable profit-making grain. It had a voracious appetite for fertilizer, thanks to the Japanese, and it thirsted for unprecedented amounts of water, while demanding herbicides and pesticides in quantities noted on the financial exchanges in New York, Zurich, and Frankfurt. Grains Americans praised made use of forty pounds of fertilizer per acre, but superwheat could take up three and almost four times as much. Yielding a dozen loaves when others could provide but one, superwheat made capital pay high returns.

The newspapers would require many years more to learn the correct spelling of Norman Borlaug's name, but the Rockefeller Foundation took notice of the man. And in 1962, linking up with Ford, the two foundations brought to prominence a New Englander named Robert Chandler, who had visions of a stunted breed of "Miracle Rice."

To be sure, wheat was the proverbial staff of life, and superwheat was the sturdiest staff of all, but rice was what most people ate. It is the staple food for more than half of mankind, and more than half of that half lives in the poor countries of the tropics. An all-tropical rice technology, comparable to that of the new wheats, could help shield much of the rest of the world from the fallout of the population explosion. In Asia, which consumes nine of every ten bowls of the world's rice and contains most of the earth's people, and where the people are multiplying faster than those of any other continent, protection of this sort seemed the best civil defense.

Ford and Rockefeller sent Chandler to Asia, 500 miles into the tropics, to the friendly Philippines. They gave him an air-conditioned laboratory, a 200-acre field beside a chain of volcanoes, and several million dollars to spend. Chandler worked fast. The payoff came in one-fifth the time it had taken pioneering Borlaug to succeed.

Chandler found a diminutive Chinese rice with the whole-tasty-meal-sounding name of *Dee-geo-woo-gen*. Somehow Dee-geo-woo-gen, which had been grown in south China for hundreds of years, had crossed the Formosa Straits to Taiwan, and now it had the good fortune to be mated by Chandler to a slender Indonesian female called *Peta*. Five rice generations later, in 1966, Chandler announced IR-8, a hardy race of blind pygmies, not half as tall as time-honored, six-foot Asian rice, but packing up to six times more for a man to eat.

Like superwheat, miracle rice could return a handsome dollar profit in chemicals, energy, and many other fields. Every pound of fertilizer applied to an acre sown to IR-8, for example, added twenty pounds of rice to the yield, doubling the output of the finest predecessor breeds—not once but three times a year. And where the old, established plants would stagger and topple over when asked to carry more than forty pounds of fertilizer on an acre, miracle rice could pile three times as much on its little back and stand straight, though never tall.

Unmindful of the season, it matured in any four months' time—thirty to sixty days sooner than the traditional varieties. This meant two significant advances. First the border at which rice could be cultivated was pushed north and south by hundreds of miles, duplicating an important feat accomplished by the Chinese in the eleventh century. Their discovery at that time of a fast-ripening rice made possible the northerly extension of paddy fields, and as a consequence, had a major influence on China's population growth and social and economic progress (miracle rice, as we shall see, is today beginning to assume a similar role in China—one of the as yet scarcely noticed and undoubtedly unintentional effects of the American-sponsored green revolution).

Second, early-maturing IR-8 freed tropical soils for an entire new crop, if not of rice, of something else, even superwheat. This made for productivity and sharp additions to the value of the land. An enterprising businessman, a landlord, and even a farmer, favored by the run of chance, could get rich, or at least richer. Such was the mood that grew in the mid-1960s as the green revolution began to spread.

The genes of miracle rice were still unassembled, when superwheat began to move. In India a young agricultural scientist named Swaminathan, only dimly aware of Borlaug's work, had reached the alarming conclusion in 1962 that his country's grain capacity was coming to a dead end.[14] He had calculated that India's wheat production, so vital to at least the *chapati*-eating north, could do nothing but stagnate. Even the most modern agricultural techniques did little to raise the food product of Indian wheats. The wheat lands of India had been yielding a steady but feeble 700 pounds of grain per acre for the past thirty years. They had no place to go forward, and when the monsoons failed, scarcity would follow. In a country with more than its share of the population explosion, he foresaw the vitiation of India as a viable state. Swaminathan wrote a letter to Borlaug.

In Pakistan two junior men, who had been trained by Borlaug, had already brought home some superwheat seeds in 1961. They had planted them on a test plot, and against the rules of their superiors, which withheld the required amounts of fertilizer, were cultivating them Mexican-style.[15] Superwheat proved itself unattached to its home ground; it grew handily. The superiors wrote a letter to Borlaug.

In 1963 Borlaug went to Pakistan and India with invitations from both governments. He sold them a few bags of seed, enough to plant twenty-five acres. When India's seeds arrived, Swaminathan's heart sank. They were unsightly and colored wrong to Indian eyes, but when planted they did well in both India and Pakistan, yielding at some trial sites five times more than the local wheats. Swaminathan began to breed reddish, Mexican superwheat (a cast reminiscent of unpopular American imports) Indian white. More seed was ordered, thirty-five truckloads for India's and Pakistan's 1965 growing season. Farmers were beginning to ask, "Where can I get some of that seed?"

On the way to the port, the thirty-five trucks got caught in the Watts riot in Los Angeles. India and Pakistan went to war against one another. Many of the seeds were damaged and spoiled at sea. Both countries were suffering a serious deterioration of food supplies. But Pakistan sowed 12,000 acres to superwheat that year, and India, 7,400. The following March (1966), as the wheats were ripening in the field, Borlaug went to Asia on an inspection tour, after which he wrote a memorandum to Pakistan's Secretary of Agriculture:

> Sir . . . One year ago we predicted that Pakistan could increase its wheat production by fifty percent in five years, and by 100 percent in eight to ten years. Six

months ago . . . we made the more optimistic forecast that wheat production could be doubled in five years. We now repeat that forecast . . .

On our recent tour of West Pakistan some officers said to us: "You must be out of your mind to predict that the wheat crop can double in five years. There has been no such change in our lifetime." Others said . . . "Pakistan cultivators are illiterate. They are slow to change."

We were not surprised by these comments. We heard the same comments in Mexico ten years ago. . . . We repeat this story not to praise Mexico, but to reassure the doubters among your agricultural officers. West Pakistan now has all the advantages which Mexico had, and more. You have the same latitude, the same irrigation, the same progressive farmers, and many of the same crops. You have saved years of research by the importation of dwarf wheat seeds. . . .

This is a revolution.[16]

Borlaug's prediction came true in 1970, that is, in four years not five, and in India the same kind of history was being made. "They may be illiterate," it was said as farmers queued for the new seeds, "but they know how to figure."

In 1966 miracle rice was introduced. Superwheat was sown to 1.5 million acres, India planting 200 times as much as the season before. Turkey, Nepal, and Afghanistan joined the revolution. But miracle rice transcended the entire phenomenon, going under 2.5 million acres of tropical soil in India, Pakistan, Laos, Malaysia, and the Philippines. The next crop-year, 16.6 million acres were growing the new grains, and when the bountiful monsoon of 1968 was flooding the rice fields of Asia, the green revolution was announced to the outside world in a now famous article by Lester Brown.

Brown, a former official of the U.S. Department of Agriculture, published his report in the July, 1968, issue of *Foreign Affairs.* He could not have found a less credulous audience, for the revival of Malthusianism was at its peak. The Paddock book, aimed at much the same readership as *Foreign Affairs,* had just come out with its message that the "impenetrable mudslide" of humanity had rendered famines of continental proportions "inevitable." [17] *The New York Times* was running advertisements quoting the former director general of the FAO declaring that the world's food supply had *already* run out for 10,000 persons daily, who were therefore dying of starvation at the rate of one "every 8.6 seconds." [18] And C. P. Snow was saying that before long "many millions of people in the poor countries are going to starve to death before our eyes . . . I have never been nearer to despair this year . . . than ever in my life." [19]

Understandably, therefore, Brown began cautiously:

> For those whose thinking of Asia is conditioned by the food crises of 1965 and 1966, the news of an agricultural revolution may come as a surprise. But the change and ferment now evident in the Asian countryside stretching from Turkey to the Philippines, and including the pivotal countries of India and Pakistan, cannot be described as anything less. . . . there is little prospect that it will abort, so powerful and pervasive are the forces behind it. . . .
>
> As of mid-1968, both the food situation and food production prospects in Asia have changed almost beyond belief.[20]

The Philippines, Brown revealed, had in a single year become self-sufficient in rice, its staple food, for the first time since 1903. Iran had achieved the status of an exporter of wheat that year. Pakistan's wheat crop was up 30 percent over its previous record; and India's 32 percent in a single year. The revolution could be repeated in Africa and Latin America, he said. If it continued, Brown concluded, "It could well become the most significant world economic development since the economic rebirth of Europe following World War II."

Some people were astounded, all the more so when former U.S. Secretary of Defense Robert McNamara, who had become president of the World Bank, stepped forward to add: "We are now on the brink of an agricultural revolution as significant as any development since the Industrial Revolution." [21]

It was at about this time that someone called the revolution "green," and the name held fast.

By 1971 most of Brown's figures had been quantified by multipliers of two and three. At least 50 million acres of tropical and subtropical lands were being cultivated the green revolution way. India, with almost half its wheat lands conquered by the dwarfs, was going into surplus production, two full years ahead of even the most carefree predictions of Borlaug and his followers. North Africa, the Middle East, parts of Latin America, and several countries of South and Southeast Asia were sowing the new seeds and harvesting bumper crops, as were nations of the Communist world. The Chinese, who were, according to Joseph Alsop, supposed to be eating human placentas to stay alive, were reporting their ninth consecutive year of record harvests. They had either somehow acquired the Rockefeller-Ford seeds or had bred their own, but almost all their subtropical rice fields were sown to the dwarf. North Vietnam had two-thirds of its rice areas planted to the Chinese dwarfs, and Cuba had 91 percent sown to IR-8, which it revealed it had obtained "*venciendo innumerables dificultades.*" [22]

Indeed IR-8 had grown obsolete, replaced by the more

efficient IR-20 and IR-22 (which in turn are rapidly becoming outmoded), and new varieties bred to specific local conditions. In India all of the Mexican wheats had been replaced by a new, still more vigorous generation of dwarfs. They had been bred Indian-fashion to a higher level of compatibility with the peculiarities of the red, crumbly plains of South Asia.

The dwarfing trick had been turned on other cereals, tropical corn for one, and the knack of yielding high was being imparted to nongrain tropical crops, such as sugarcane and cotton. High-yielding tropical chickens and cows were coming along, and the genes of the fathering dwarf wheats were being rewound with knowledge about how to increase their protein-making capacity. The first man-made supergrain was under development. It was called *Triticale,* a dwarf—half wheat, half rye—yielding higher than the best of both in protein and in weight.

Overnight fortunes were made on the green revolution. In India, for example, profits sometimes ran as high as 100 percent return on investment. Industry moved capital into tropical agriculture. Land values soared. Jobs opened up, notably for the teeming landless farmhands, who make up such a great part of the "population bomb." And among those peasants who did own land, a rural class of *nouveau riche* suddenly appeared. Even the poorest peasant, if he possessed only a single hectare of irrigable land, was given a scheme worked out by agricultural economists by which the green revolution might provide him with a steady income five times higher than he had made in any previous year.

More important than anything else, the precipitate changes wrought by the dwarfs and all they signified had produced a new social consciousness among the rural people.

Many had been drawn from static subsistence farming into the upward whirl of a market economy, a glittering palace whence few have ever willingly returned.

All sorts of strategies were drawn. A star had been born. The FAO made the new seeds a "spearhead to development" in its master "Indicative World Plan" for agriculture.[23] It catapulted the spread of the green revolution to first place among the tasks necessary for economic and social betterment in the Third World. Governments and establishments in general agreed. Many of them saw the new phenomenon as a kind of gold coin with which a full blink of historic time might be bought. The coming of the famines, which had been seen as an approaching high-speed train, had been slowed at an unexpected whistle stop. Suddenly there seemed to be a way to restrain the "impenetrable mudslide."

When the 1970s began, however, it had already become clear that the time purchased would fall much shorter than that for which they had bargained. The green revolution was racing into the tangles of a finite social structure, and it began to lose pace. Rapid change ran headlong into hard tradition. The green revolution was creating new difficulties, a series of "second generation problems."

Few people could doubt the enormous capacities of the dwarf races, but they had burst upon the scene so abruptly as to unsettle old equilibriums. The buildup of a glut of food surpluses was being forecast now. This could seriously upset the world market. Indeed, grain prices began to fall, which had the effect of both knocking the wind out of the running dwarfs and reinforcing the recessionary process. Worse, it was said, surpluses invariably lead to a reduction of farm acreage and, as an unavoidable consequence, a shift to the cities of rural populations. In the unindustrialized, heavily populated tropics, this would mean an immense rise in unemployment. The wealth created by the green revolution would thus accrue only to the already wealthy, while the inefficient, have-nothing peasant masses were doomed to failure and displacement to the seething shantytowns, which even now were closing like a noose around the cities. With the discontented and dispossessed shoehorned into the physical proximity of political power, violent social upheaval was foreordained. The green revolution, some were quick to say, was bound to turn red.

Then, ecologists began to warn that the dwarf races were untried by time. What if they should fall victim to some unknown disease? With their rapid diffusion across the continents, a global catastrophe would ensue. In any event, Malthusians recalled, the doubling, tripling, and quadrupling of agricultural production would only increase human numbers. It would also, others maintained, lead to a tremendous escalation of harmful chemicals entering the biosphere. In the end the green revolution would yield less, not more, food than before, as the soils would be hopelessly ruined. The ticking of the population bomb and cries of crime in the streets were held close to the ear.

Ehrlich called the green revolution "make-believe," and those who did not think so "clowns."[24] William Paddock said it was all a "cruel joke"[25]; it "could do us all in—if it worked."

Was the green revolution a cornucopia or a Pandora's box?

The question was raised, once again in *Foreign Affairs,* by agriculturalist Clifton Wharton.[26] He warned that the "quiet, passive peasant is already aware of the modern world—far more than we realize—and he is impatient to gain his share." The green revolution offered him "the dramatic possibility of achieving his goal," while it had caught many unawares. The time had come, he urged, "to engage in contingency planning so that we may respond flexibly and quickly as the Revolution proceeds." This has in fact been done, but Wharton's further admonition to place the green revolution in its long-range perspective has gone virtually unheeded. Such an effort, it would seem, requires the development of many points of view and some knowledge of how wide the new technologies may extend.

The breakthrough in plant genetics that led to the green revolution represents an advance in a small corner of a single scientific discipline. But presently there is a multitude of such corners in many of the sciences, and this has mighty implications for the giant in the earth. Powered by varied and sometimes conflicting intentions, scientists are engaged in highly diverse tasks, which seem to foreshadow a golden age in food culture for all mankind, whatever its numbers may be.

The dwarfs by themselves offer the countries of the tropics the means of producing their staple foods at a rate that comfortably exceeds the highest pace of population growth. In South and Southeast Asia, for example, food production in 1970 was 5 percent higher than the previous year—about twice the region's rate of population increase. Yet the offering is but a taste of what lies ahead.

In 1967, then U.S. Secretary of Agriculture Orville Freeman gave a series of talks in which he sketched twenty-first century agriculture. Reporting on the year 2000, he saw the United States as an uncrowded, unstrained nation—though 50 percent more populated than it is today—being fed better than ever by push-button farming, with machines pushing the buttons.[27] Tomorrow's farmers, he said, "relieved at last of the physical drudgery and occupational anxiety so traditionally theirs," will sit at a desk interpreting data transmitted by a network of space satellites. This sophisticated hardware, equipped with remote sensing equipment, will provide a constant supply of millions of information bits about soils, crops, weather, etc., to a land-based computer center, which in turn will decide what, when, and how to plant, harvest, and market.

Cattle will eat less and grow fatter, he said, hens will lay almost twice as many eggs as now, cornstalks will have multiple ears, and cotton bolls will cluster at the top of the plant for easy, automated picking. Drought will be an unfamiliar word, crop diseases will be preventable, and all the hated pesticides will no longer be in use; for America is to be a sanitary place, completely insect-free ("Americans of the year 2000 never will see—much less swat—a housefly or a mosquito").

Freeman's look into the future was hardly far-fetched. That same year, in fact, the USDA signed contracts with NASA for the use of satellites in farming; and the launching of computerized, spaceborne remote sensors to help increase agricultural and fishing yields is years, not decades, away. Moreover, most of Freeman's predictions are already more or less foregone conclusions, to be realized if not by the year 2000 then within the next half century, and not simply for America but for the entire world. And there is much he omitted.

Upgrading conventional agriculture is dependent on four main technologies, all of which are flourishing. These are genetic engineering, mechanization, irrigation, and the chemical control of plant growth through fertilizers and weed and insect killers. They are associated with an array of other activities ranging from molecular biology to nuclear physics, from space science to geology, from oceanography to meteorology, from education to synthetic and frozen foods. From a review of the documentation in these fields, it is possible to construct a scenario of what agriculture might be like fifty or sixty years from now, or sooner.[28]

Such a leap into the third millennium A.D. was recently undertaken in a paper prepared by the FAO's top futurologist, Walter H. Pawley, director of the organization's Policy Advisory Bureau. Looking specifically toward the latter part of the next century, he foresaw a fiftyfold increase in food production, feeding a greatly expanded world population "on a diet similar to that now prevailing in North America or Northwestern Europe." [29] He conditioned his calculations on the proviso that two technical breakthroughs be made—"both of which would seem to be a distinct possibility long before 100 years have elapsed," he said.[30] These were: a method for the cultivation of tropical soils now covered by forest; and economically feasible desalinization of seawater and its delivery inland.

On the basis of Pawley's study and other material, let us venture only as far as, say, 2030, so that we can in the same instance celebrate the one hundredth anniversary of the failure of the great English chemist-inventor Sir William Cooke's prophecy in 1899 of global starvation by 1930.

It is the time of universal irrigation, the dispersion of purified water in such a way as to immerse the entire planet in the cool bath that gives life to all organic things. Men have learned to extract valuable metals and minerals from the oceans, giving desalinization a cost factor of zero. and with the installation of thermal pumps powered by the sun, the water runs across hundreds of miles and uphill, wherever it can serve. Fertilizers, as they were earlier known, are gone; plants are being bred to fertilize themselves, but for now the water itself has been enriched with all the required nutrients, which are borne in time capsules activated at the very moment and in the precise quantity the demands of growth require. Gone, too, are useless weeds. Gone are the germs of plant disease. And gone are the insects that attack the foods of man, victims of bacteriological and viral agents evolved by human hands.

Now, to take one example of the effect all this has had, the Sahara Desert, an area almost equal to the world's total cultivated land in the 1970s, is, in 2030, in the process of becoming a single tropical garden. It is now possible to extend farmland five times that of the Sahara. But the Sahara by itself has been rendered capable—if necessary—of growing all the food needed by the 15 billion people who inhabit the earth in 2030, for molecular biologists and plant geneticists have replaced all the old generations of plants with new crops attuned to man's needs and inclinations.

A combination of highly specific, radiation-induced mutations and genetic surgery performed with the scalpel of laser beams has made plants obedient to men, not to chance. In the late 1960s geneticists concerned about swiftly growing numbers of the planet's poor had argued the case for implanting men with the genes for a two-compartment stomach. With this equipment man—like a cow, which has four such enclosures—would have been able to digest the cellulose in paper and sawdust and all the protein-rich, but inedible, fibrous leaves that abounded in the tropics. But more thoughtful—and perhaps somewhat more sentimental—men turned their knowledge on the leaves themselves and made them compatible with less efficient stomachs, although by 2030 leaf-eating has long since been forgotten.

More important, they concentrated on the things men like to eat, creating familiar plants with remarkable productive capacities and qualities of nutrition that far exceeded their ancestral strains. By a process called fusion, first demonstrated in the 1960s, the genetic material of widely divergent plants was made to come together and generate new breeds. Thus all important crops were given the ability of pulses—plants such as peas, beans, and lentils—to tap free nitrogen in the air, and thereby fertilize themselves and obviate the need for chemical additions to the soil. Disease resistance was transferred from one plant to another, eliminating all disease, and, for example, the proteins of rice, once lost in the milling, were moved to the center of the kernel. And the genes of every plant that grows manufacture all the proteins healthy men require.

Freeman's satellites have long ago been taken down and shelved. The advances described above, and the mastery of weather, made them obsolete. Space stations in the distant sky now orbit the moon and the planets, surveying the incipient agriculture men have undertaken there for experimental purposes, for a great program has been launched to unlock the remaining secrets of photosynthesis.

Obsolete, too, for reasons of their superfluousness, are all the unconventional and synthetic foods developed in the latter half of the twentieth century by a community that felt lingering anxiety about its future food supply. Relatively few people ever had to eat hydrolyzed cellulose, cultured plankton and algae, and the single-cell proteins made in the 1970s from low-grade petroleum—though all had been rendered highly nutritious and tasty to even the most discriminating tongue. Multitiered hydroponics—plants grown in soil-free tanks, which rotate toward the sun—proved to be unnecessary, too, though the husbanding rather than hunting of fish, which began to multiply yields when first practiced on a wide scale fifty years ago, still fills a certain need. Not needed at all, however, are the simulated soya steaks, and the synthetic proteins once added to soft drinks and common table salt; now, good nutrition rides free on every morsel of all the favored foods.

The new "agriculture" of 2030 is the new antiagriculture—the ushering in of the third great age of man: post-agricultural primary production. Men had been hunters for 100,000 years, and farmers for only one-tenth that time, but farming has long been an anachronism. Even a century ago one man and his machines making, say, steel could turn out in a single day more of his finished product than one man and his land might produce in an entire year. With the advent of advanced technology in both farming and industry, the imbalance has hardly been adjusted. But as early as 1902 the celebrated botanist Gottlieb Haberlandt had foretold that it might one day be possible to bypass the entire vegetative process and propagate unlimited populations of genetically identical individual plants from a single cell of a single parent.

The method, which is called "cloning," was first accomplished in the 1940s in experiments at Cornell University. Cells from the root of a carrot were made to reproduce at the astonishing speed of five times their own weight per day. Fulfilling Haberlandt's prophecy, they multiplied not mere copies of their kind but began to reconstruct flawless duplicates of the entire carrot from which they had been excised.

What was done for the carrot was later done for other plants, notably the group containing food grains. By 1970 a frog had been cloned, and men began to see that human beings could be created asexually, each individual made anew in countless numbers, hatched in an artificial womb.

Every single cell of every living thing contains all the genetic information necessary to produce the whole organism, and as every plant is made of cells by the many millions, in such numbers might man produce his food. The significance of cloning plants, not to mention other forms of life, is that land can be freed from food production, and if we use the rate of growth achieved in the 1940s, the results cannot but astound. An acre sown to the miracle rice of the 1970s yields two tons of grain in 120 days, but if this population were cloned, ten tons would be produced every day of every year. A kind of fermentation industry would be installed in space infinitesimally smaller than all the cultivated lands, and every food known to man would be made in any number, with every quality desired. All the land once stripped and plowed could be given back to nature, all the yearned-for features of the primordial environment restored.

Only faultless knowledge of the unknown qualities of photosynthesis could rival such a system. Then, with food production (if food is needed still) based on building from a simple inorganic pile, man will have thrown his saddle on the sun.

All this is not an idle dream. The research is now under way. The forward momentum is there. But there are barriers.

II

THE POPULATION IMPERATIVE

THE PERFORMANCE OF superwheat and miracle rice, and the penetrative advance of the new technologies, demand a review of the population problem.[1] There are many reasons for doing so, among them the compelling fact that the green revolution is spreading faster than people are being born.

The world population, for the past decade or so, has been growing at about 2 percent a year. It is rarely recalled that the average annual increase since the discovery of agriculture has been only .003 percent, a progression that would require more than 23,000 years for the number of people to double again. But this is because there now appears to be no chance in the foreseeable future that the average will be restored.

If the present rate were to continue, the inviolable laws of exponential growth decree that in another thousand years there would be roughly 1,000,000,000,000,000,000 (1 billion billion) people, that is, 175 men, women and children for every square foot of the earth's surface including the oceans, the jungles, and the poles. You would have 52,500 uninvited persons in a 15- × 20-foot living room, sixty of whom would have to stand on your toes, three people to the head of a pin. Thirty-seven years later, all the figures, save the dimensions of the living room, your toes, and the pin, would have doubled.

Although, for obvious reasons, only the most boisterous demographers carry out the logic of their projections for so many years, this, as everyone knows, is called the population explosion. It is a simple numbers game that has a powerful effect on anyone who has ever ridden in a crowded subway car or had to queue for an hour to see a film. But the game can be played in more than one way, where the numbers amuse and even enlighten rather than scare.

Few countries in the world of the ten- or fifteen-year-old population explosion are growing in numbers as fast as the United States did in the seventy-year period between 1790 and 1860. At that time, population bombs were not yet invented, but during that period the annual rate was almost 3.5 percent. Had the pace continued, America would now be the most populous place in the world, containing eight times its present numbers, and more than twice that of China. In the year 2000 there would be 4 billion Americans, and in 2160, nearly a thousand years in advance of the schedules worked out today, the count would surpass one trillion.

But as America has now only 12 percent of the number of people for which there were strong grounds to predict a little over a century ago, something must have happened after 1860 to slow the whole thing down. Since then, in fact, in spite of the mass immigration that followed the Civil War, the rate has fallen rather steadily, once halved, then halved again.

The truth is that men as yet have failed to understand fully why populations grow. To explain the sharp inclines we see today in the poor countries, some cite the obvious: as modern medicine and health care go forward, life spans widen, and fewer people die every year, while birth rates have yet to change. But this does little to clarify the situation in the United States and all the nations of wealth. There, death rates decrease very little, but birth rates have fallen, and so these countries are increasing in numbers relatively slowly. For them, it is said, and it is undoubtedly true, where education expands, birth rates contract, and the growth of well-being makes family sizes decline.

But all this is a partial explanation, hardly a theory, which must dispose of every question. It is useful for only the most recent events, and it cannot be assuredly foretold that the present excess in births over deaths will by education, or anything else that is known, recede to zero. Moreover, nobody entirely knows why populations grew in the centuries before the "explosion," when death rates were high all over, and well-being was universally low.

The Rev. Thomas Robert Malthus, one of the world's most despondent men, thought he had the answer—at least until he got older and his own bottomless despair made him wary of the great message he advanced (an episode little remembered now).[2] Malthus, who exercised a powerful influence on his generation and those that followed, particularly ours, was thirty-two years old when in 1798 he published anonymously the first edition of *An Essay on the Principle of Population as it Affects the Future Improvement of Society, with Remarks on the Speculations of Mr. Godwin, M. Condorcet, and Other Writers.* Most of the Malthusians of today, the neo-Malthusians, no longer advocate quite the same proposals favored by the Great Pessimist himself (such as workhouses for the poor), and Malthus would be appalled by the suggestions of his modern disciples (he was categorically against birth control). But all the neo-Malthusians are in accord with the essential elements of his famous theory, which has gained in acceptance with the passage of time.

Until Malthus, many people thought population growth was a good thing. To be sure, Pope Urban II in 1095 launched his Crusaders against the "wicked race" with the following words: "The land which you inhabit . . . is too narrow for your large population . . . it furnishes scarcely enough food for its cultivators."[3] But Adam Smith wrote before Malthus that "the most decisive mark of the prosperity of any country is the increase of the number of its inhabitants,"[4] and the post-Columbian era was one of general confidence in the bountifulness of earth.

But Malthus, writing under the impact of the European population explosion (1750–1850), when his own country's food supplies were growing scarce, saw a nexus between people and their primary nourishment in which, as the Paddocks later put it, the stork must inevitably outpace the plow. Malthus believed he had discovered the general laws of population growth, and he stated them with admirable simplicity.

All hopes for human happiness cannot but come to naught, Malthus said, for populations in whatever time or place always increase beyond the very limits to which people can be fed, and there they are held behind the unremovable bars of famine, poverty, and disease. For every advance made in food production, he maintained, larger numbers of people would soon come along to annul it, for the only checks on population were "vice and misery."

By "misery" he meant war, starvation, and sickness, and

in "vice" he included contraception, of which he never spoke, he said, "without the most marked disapprobation." [5] Thus the lot of mankind was to be wretched indeed.

The theoretical basis of Malthus' conclusions was founded solely on his insight that while populations may grow in geometric progression, food production could be increased only in arithmetic progression. It was another way of saying that the addition of one man and woman to the population can eventually produce unlimited numbers of people—through their children, grandchildren, and so on—while the addition of one piece of cultivated land, no matter the size, can yield only a limited amount of more food, whatever it may be.

This is certainly true, but it is a long jump to finding that more food is the *cause* of more people, and the ground underneath has been carefully chipped away. Yet it remains the view of the neo-Malthusians, and one among them, economist-ecologist, sometimes-humorist Kenneth Boulding of the University of Colorado has broadened it to all-inclusive dimensions. Boulding, whose wry wit much improves on the sobriety of Malthus, calls his proposition the "Utterly Dismal Theorem." He is grimly serious, however, when he goes on to affirm

> that if the only check on growth of population is starvation and misery, then any technological improvement will have the ultimate effect of increasing the sum of human misery as it permits a larger proportion to live in precisely the same state of misery and starvation as before the change.[6]

Not much can be said in favor of this "theorem." On the other hand, there is now a great deal of evidence to show that if there is an axis linking food to population growth, Malthus and his latter-day followers have got the connection standing on its head.

It is not an increase in food supplies that *causes* populations to grow, although it obviously sustains higher numbers. It is the other way around: *An increase in population causes food supplies to grow.*

This idea is not new. Sir James Steuart advanced it, rather weakly, in the eighteenth century, but Malthus said, as was his style whenever he did not agree, that Sir James had "fallen in an error."[7] Malthus then went on to "prove" that agriculture was the "efficient cause" of population, and Sir James, presumably intimidated, was never heard from again. Malthus maintained that the order of which came first, an increase in food or an increase in population, was "the hinge on which the subject turns." But why populations expand, in spite of Malthus, remains an unanswered social riddle, and why people live in misery and vice cannot be meaningfully correlated to farming, much as some might prefer to do so rather than to ask more searching questions. Green revolutions do not make more people. It is people who are forced by their numbers, in opposition to their deepest inclinations, to undertake the heavy labor of improving productivity. Population growth powers social change. It may be the strongest engine of all.

The reason for this is remarkably uncomplicated. Let the credit for sound theories fall to a Danish economist named Ester Boserup, who in a much neglected essay made it plain for anyone to see. Her thesis, displayed in a brief book, *The Conditions of Agricultural Growth,* first published in 1965, is based on the convincing observation that men do not generally work harder than they must, that given the drudgery of farming this is particularly true, and that tradition and the habits of centuries are a mighty chain to put asunder.[8]

The essence of Boserup's idea is that it was not possible that any people might engage themselves in an effort that would require an increase in physical work to yield the same amount of food as they could produce by less toil. Yet the advance from lower to higher forms of agriculture, at least for a considerable time, *always* demands precisely this kind of intensification of labor. The explanation of this is as follows.

Agriculture usually starts in the forest. Any given territory of forest cannot support a hunting economy with a human population density of more than ten persons for every square mile. When the density rises above that figure, farming, when it is known, begins to take over, and the common first step—still practiced today in some parts of the world by more than 200 million people—is the clearing of forest growth by burning. When the fires go out a loose, arable soil remains, enriched by the fertilizing dust of the ash of burned trees. Such soil is easily tilled with a simple digging stick. Farming requires only a few hours' work here and there, and is far from becoming a daily routine. After a year or two, however, the land loses its fertility, and the farmer must clear another area of forest, which serves for an equal period. The exhausted soil is left to recover, and if it lies fallow for twenty to twenty-five years, it becomes forest once again.[9]

After a quarter of a century the process can then be repeated, but when the population density rises to a higher level, and more food is to be produced, the fallow period must be shortened, and a new stage of agriculture imperceptibly sets in. The land no longer has time enough to regain a cover of forest, and when fallow drops below ten years, the soil laid to rest is blanketed not with trees but with bush. The clearing of bush bares soil much more compact than before. The stick gives way to the hoe. Weeding becomes an arduous task. Yet the farmer continues to enjoy long periods when there is no work to do; but as his clan gets larger, the fallow period grows shorter still. The gradual enslavement to the soil proceeds. The cycle goes on to the next phase, then the next, then the next, a transformation normally requiring many centuries. At last, all the land has long ago been cleared and is under constant cultivation. The farmer, rising with the sun, must day to day hitch his flesh to the hated iron plow.

On the other hand, Boserup has recorded, in cases where population density has been reduced by war or other means, farmers have reverted to less laborious systems of cultivation.[10] Further, in contradiction to Malthusian theory, many populations that have declined have never regained their numbers in spite of their knowledge of intensive agricultural techniques (which were abandoned and eventually forgotten), as with the Indians of post-Columbian Latin America.

Thus, it is only by the most dire necessity—the loss of a people's capacity to feed their children, as a result of population growth—that they consent to alter long-ingrained life patterns and escalate the working day.

The history of agriculture has been the history of this painful process, and that is why the peasant, since he first appeared, is almost everywhere regarded as low on the social scale, meriting mockery and scorn. The farmer is low in the Indian castes, and primitive people, anthropology has repeatedly shown, usually consider hunting, fishing, and food-gathering as pleasurable endeavors, while agriculture is looked on as an abominable grind, the last resort of the hungriest man.[11]

Once it is demonstrated that it is the addition of more human beings that brings about improvements in agriculture, and not the other way around, the origins of the present green revolution become clear. More important the problems associated with today's population explosion can be seen in greater depth.

Many writers have referred to the discovery of agriculture and the social changes that ensued as revolutionary, and, with hindsight, it most assuredly was. But it took place in an age in which populations grew extremely slowly, and any contemporary observer could scarcely have detected much progress in the modes of food production within a single lifetime. In the same way that man is denied sight of the slow rise of great mountains, he would have been unable to see the impalpable dynamic of agriculture, and might have called it a stagnant economy without much of a future. With a few exceptions, notably in Europe and the United States in the nineteenth and twentieth centuries, later witnesses might have made similar notations—as, in fact, they did. Today, however, the same transformation cannot fail to be noticed, because it has been greatly accelerated. Population growth is "exploding" at a speed 667 times the historic average, and this has created tremendous pressure on the social system.

Changes that once took place over a thousand years are now occurring in a year and a half; for what might have been done in a century, today less than two months can be spared. When an Indian farmer in one season sinks an irrigation well, plants the seeds of the green revolution, and then goes on to grow three or four crops a year, he is only keeping one stride ahead of the pace, but the power of social change grows in all those who cannot do so.

The rising densities of population are making vast

claims on the way things have too long been done. In the agriculture of the world's poor countries, where alterations must come first, this means radical changes in land tenure, income distribution, and a general assault on the keepers of a nation's wealth. It is an affront to old, established interests, but it also means that all the dispossessed, who by their numbers raise the challenge, must themselves conform to the stern demands of high-speed population growth. Until now, peasants accused of laziness were in fact, as studies have consistently revealed, only acting in a rational manner.[12] But there is a new rationality growing out of the green revolution, which impels them to break with tired old traditions and get accustomed quickly to hard and useful work. In short, the whole social structure is being shaken by a human quake, and if the epicenter lies in the underdeveloped world, the shock waves are global.

It is therefore only natural that some raise the problems of growing population as a specter, but when the question of food supplies is divorced from a causal relationship with "vice and misery," it becomes clear that the fears can only be greatest among those who wish to preserve the Old Order. Undoubtedly there are pockets of overpopulation in many places of the world, and knowledge of birth-control technology is a great social liberator for both women and men, which ought to be extended as a universal human right. But the sores of overly concentrated areas (mostly cities) can respond to sociological treatment, and contraception is not an independent variable, nor can it be legislated or otherwise regulated to achieve worldwide zero population growth.

In the first place, birth-control education yields diminishing returns. Once the bedroom secrets of family planning are learned, there is nothing more to know. Even if contraception were to be practiced worldwide, and couples could somehow be acculturated to desire only two children—that is, enough human beings to replace themselves—population would eventually decline sharply, since many women do not or cannot have children and a certain number of offspring die before reaching the age of fertility. No country can be in favor of a falling population for very long; a 1 percent drop below zero growth, if uncorrected, would cause the human race to vanish within a millennium. Thus people would have to be made to want three children. But that is too much, and and as no one can have a number of children between two and three, the population would continue to grow. Some families must therefore be allowed three or even four children, and as one observer asked recently, "Who is to select these families, and on what basis?"[13]

Furthermore, were zero growth attainable by other means—Ehrlich suggests adding sterilants to the water supplies or to staple foods ("Doses of the antidote would be carefully rationed by the government to produce the desired population size")[14]—this, too, would be undesirable. In the United States a vocal group of population lobbyists has been calling for ZPG,[15] but the Rockefeller Presidential Commission on Population Growth and the American Future is dubious. Reporting to the President in 1971, the commission outlined some of the effects ZPG would have in America. To achieve zero growth, it said, couples would at once have to limit their childbearing to an average of one, because of the age structure of the present U.S. population. It continued:

> Ten years from now the population under ten years old would be only forty-three percent of what it now

> is, with disruptive effects on the school system and ultimately on the number of persons entering the labor force. Thereafter, a constant total population could be maintained only if this small generation in turn had two children and their grandchildren had nearly three children on the average. And then the process would again have to reverse, so that the overall effect for many years would be that of an accordion-like mechanism requiring continuous expansion and contraction.
>
> We doubt that such consequences are intended by the advocates of immediate zero population growth.* [16]

In the fragile underdeveloped countries, where most people live and are multiplying much faster than the present world median, such spasms would be unbearable. Under heavy demographic pressure, the world is rapidly expanding its productive capacities, and any sudden turnabout would be economically and socially intolerable. On reflection no one can really want ZPG; as the French demographer Alfred Sauvy has noted, "The historian cannot show us any example of population stagnation or decline whose results have been happy." [17] It is true that a slowdown in growth would alleviate stress on the social order, but it is far from certain that such relief is a good thing, since to the extent that the pressure to change is reduced, the iniquitous status quo may be retained.

Further, higher population densities, as has often been demonstrated, permit higher economies, and geometric in-

* Nevertheless the consequences are even now being felt, mainly as a result of the efforts of the neo-Malthusian population controllers. Childbearing in the United States, according to a 1971 report by the Washington Center for Metropolitan Studies, is declining at a record rate, which could have severe repercussions on the nation's "growth-oriented" economy. The report said that there were 15.5 percent fewer children under five years of age in 1970 than in 1960, and that the effects of the trend are already apparent in declining sales by the toy industry and in surplus classroom space.

creases in productivity[18]—though this is not the only determining factor. True enough, the richest countries have the lowest rates of population growth, but they have already undergone their population explosion; furthermore, their riches have much to do with the steady transfer to their coffers of wealth from the underdeveloped world since colonial times. It is not true, however, that the countries with the highest population growth rates are the poorest. Indeed, many demographers have shown that the most impressive economic advances in the Third World are being made where population densities are increasing fastest.[19] Colin Clark, for example, has demonstrated that high population growth in the underdeveloped countries encourages enterprise, results in economies in the use of capital, raises the rate of savings, and reduces the proportion of pensioners.[20] In India, he points out, the rate of savings to net national product was 5 percent in the 1950s and has now gone up to 12 percent. Concerning the green revolution, the FAO's Indicative World Plan makes it quite plain as to what is driving it forward. "There appears to be," says IWP, "a strong correlation between progress in these matters and between size and pressure of population . . ."[21] Harold J. Barnett of Washington University shares this view. In an article entitled "Population Problems—Myths and Realities" he states: "The fact is that, in virtually all of the developed or developing nations for which we have long-term economic growth data, increases in economic output per capita . . . almost always have accompanied increases in population."[22] As agrarian specialist Xavier-André Florès has noted, if the Netherlands' population density were reduced to that of the Congo, its agriculture would be completely underdeveloped, and if a global land reform were suddenly to be launched, population densities in many areas of the Third World would have to be increased.[23]

One of the reasons that cities are greater than the sum of their parts is compactness. Ease of transportation, communications, and social contact, as well as facile access to life support and other services such as hospitals, education, and the arts, make for higher forms of civilization. They open the way to the rounding of the mind and greater contributions from individuals to the commonweal. Areas of falling population density tend to become isolated zones, with declining standards of living.

In agriculture, recent research has made clear that with the increase of population density the rate of development is speeded because, in the words of one such study, "more pressure is forced upon people to adapt themselves better to the rising shortage of resources by making more use of organizational and technical progress."[24] The famines of the past occurred because the food-providing rural population was too small and too far away to provide food for the cities; these famines were due to overurbanization, not overpopulation.[25]

Malthus himself, at a later age, expressed fears about population control. He lived in a time when modern contraception technology was unknown, but he anticipated it, warning in the 1817 edition of his book:

> If it were possible for each married couple to limit by a wish the number of their children, there is certainly reason to fear that the indolence of the human race would be very greatly increased, and that neither the population of individual countries nor of the whole earth would ever reach its proper and natural extent.[26]

The danger of hysterical campaigns against population growth is greater than the threat of overpopulation itself.

It cheapens life, leading to interpretations of human beings as "impenetrable mudslides," and "tidal waves," as a series of advertisements in *The New York Times* put it repeatedly.[27] In a recent article by a high official of the FAO, people were no longer people; they were terrifying time bombs, torrents, rising floods, waves, deluges, and avalanches.[28] Philip Hauser, a demographer trying to be funny, has pointed out the advantages of cannibalism as a means of family planning.[29] It would serve the dual purpose, he said, of decreasing the population and adding to the food supply.

In the spring of 1971, when the Bengalis of what was then East Pakistan were being slaughtered at a rate in excess of that of the Jews during World War II, few words of protest were raised in the West, and nothing at all was done.* How much of this may be attributed to the general feeling that there are "too many Asians anyway," as one Bengali remarked sarcastically to me at the time, may be an unanswerable question, but we have the words of William Paddock and Robert Ardrey, as examples, and the policies of advanced nations, to attest to the fact that men and governments are not entirely averse to reducing populations by an increase in death rates.

"Good Samaritans," Paddock wrote in 1970, lamenting reports that public health practices have lowered death rates in the poor countries ("a disturbing experience"), "might well have been advised to slow down the dissemination of modern medicine [in Asia] . . . Obviously without effective population control, an agricultural breakthrough resulting in increased yields might be as detrimental to

* Of course, nothing was done for the Jews either, but their lives had also been devalued, not by the myths of the population explosion but by something equally antihuman—worldwide anti-Semitism.

some countries as was the use of DDT on the malaria anopheles mosquito." [30] DDT virtually eliminated that lethal disease in the tropics, but it seems the tropics, in the view of Paddock and many others—like Nobelist Macfarlane Burnet, who feels the elimination of infectious disease to be "disastrously short sighted" [13]—are a part of the world unprepared for life.

Ardrey is a non-Malthusian population controller, of which there appear to be very few. He is aware that, "Contrary to all of our assumptions since the days of Thomas Malthus, animal populations do not build up their numbers to that point where they encounter the veto of exhausted food supply." [32] He recalls that there are innumerable, though unexplainable, examples of many species that keep well within the carrying capacity of their habitat, but excludes or misses the possibility that the human population may be moving to its higher numbers in the same way. Instead, equating man to the animal exceptions to this rule, such as the rodents lemmings and snowshoe hares, he concludes that our kind already "stands in violation of that natural law dictating the self-regulation of animal numbers." Thus, it seems, he cannot steer clear of the familiar notion that "birth control must be compulsory." And of this comes the following unfelicitous prediction:

> We shall come, though perhaps not for a generation, to an acceptance of compulsory population restriction and to means by which it may be enforced. . . . We shall see automobile accidents as a most excellent consequence of population density, particularly in its elimination of members of the young breeding group. We shall come to take a brand-new view of homosexuality, a most dependable means of reducing breeding numbers, and of suicide itself, in highest

> praiseworthiness among the young. We shall take a new view of drugs, especially the killers like heroin. We shall recognize that pornography has its virtues, satisfying with voyeurism what otherwise might find its outlet in copulation.

I have been told in New Delhi by an officer of the United States Agency for International Development (AID) that in the early 1960s, when America was conducting a sizable health program and malaria-prevention campaign in India, economists in Washington one day declared, "Hey, why should we help lower their death rate, when they have such a population problem?" The economists in question, according to the AID, informant, were the policy-makers of the agency. This story is not verifiable, but in fact AID funds for population control rose from $2 million in 1965 to $100 million in 1971, while the agency undertook a massive pullout from all activities that lower death rates in the poor countries.[33] In India, AID population-control funding went from zero in 1965 to $20 million in 1970, and all assistance to health went to zero.[34] AID, which now shows a distinct lack of interest in bringing modern medicine to countries that still have high death rates, is not alone. Private agencies, such as the Rockefeller and Ford foundations, have withdrawn from the health business, and the Ford Foundation has suggested the reason why: "The demographic effects of modernization have been largely unintended." [35]

One might properly question the humanitarian rhetoric with which donor governments and foundations vest themselves when they go before the public. Some people who wish to plan their families may be grateful for the 144 million free condoms America sent overseas from 1968 to

1970; some are undoubtedly thankful for the sterilizations, particularly because they are often given a bonus in cash or kind to undergo the operation. But only a very few can be appreciative when their families are planned by death.* Our commitment to that sort of development assistance is not a big step from genocide.

Fortunately, in this regard at least, the Third World until now has generally not been in a buying mood for U.S. preoccupations with the population explosion. Believing that the advantages of demographic growth and high population densities outweigh the disadvantages, many underdeveloped countries remain pronatalist, in spite of much sales talk in the West and not a little arm-twisting. Explaining this vew at a recent population conference at the California Institute of Technology, James Hooker, an American Africanist scholar, said of his studies in Malawi:

> The arguments for population control in the Third World are dubious at best when they come from our mouths, and particularly suspect when they are directed at a country which by serious effort is changing its situation. Malawians, after all, are not wasting half the world's resources [an allusion to the well-known statistic that the U.S. with 6 percent of the world's population is consuming annually 50–60 percent of the yearly output of the world's nonrenewable resources].

* The poor countries are not the only ones that suffer from the death-orientation aspects of population control. Writing in the magazine of the Center for the Study of Democratic Institutions, of Santa Barbara, California, biologist Bernard Strehler has complained bitterly about a national "scandal of neglect," which surrounds the meager funds being made available for research on aging. Science, he says, is on the threshold of learning how to stretch the *healthy middle age* of life by fifteen to thirty years. But in spite of the major research effort called for by a panel of experts at the 1960 White House Conference on Aging, the funds have not been forthcoming, principally because it would add to the population explosion, though only temporarily.

> Indeed, from their view, they are increasing the globe's supply of consumables (by emphasizing agricultural development). They cannot be persuaded that life is getting worse. Discussion of the "quality of life," which so pervades American journals, seems singularly grotesque here. Americans have persuaded themselves that man has overrun the universe. In this part of Africa that assumption is rather silly.[36]

Malawians are not much taken with what appears to be "old-styled racism tricked out in new garb," he added, although that country has a population growth estimated at 3.3 percent per year, and a density four times that of Africa as a whole.

In any event, it is generally recognized that population control is a long way from becoming effective [37] and that the world's people are bound to multiply at one fast-motion speed or another. Indeed, some demographers question whether present-day contraceptive technology has any value whatsoever. At the Caltech conference referred to above, Jon McLin reported that while Belgium has one of the lowest rates of population growth in the world, the majority of Belgian couples still use *coitus interruptus* and the rhythm method to prevent conception.[38] And population economist Alan Sweezy added:

> In this respect Belgium is fairly typical of western Europe, where the greatest decline in fertility of the nineteenth and twentieth centuries came about without extensive use of even appliance methods of contraception. The modern methods, pill and IUD [intrauterine device], were of course unknown until long after the decline had reached its low point.[39]

The population of this planet is heading swiftly toward

a new equilibrium, at a number much higher than today's. No one doubts this, though the figure is often contested. In the end the population will probably expand to Malthus' "proper and natural extent" and, perhaps in the same manner that some animal populations have been shown to grow rapidly under favorable conditions and then inexplicably stabilize, will remain there for all time.

Scientist L. M. Cook, in his recent book *Coefficients of Natural Selection*, makes very clear that the growth and decline of populations, including the human race, proceed according to rules that emerge from the way living matter is organized. The *Times* of London, commenting on Cook's work, concludes that population growth is thus "a problem in natural selection and is as far outside conscious human control as any other large scale natural process." It continues:

> The point is that the so-called "population explosion," with extrapolation of indefinite exponential growth until we are all pressed tightly together is a myth. A human society, if it is technologically advanced, will arrive at whatever saturation density of population best suits the comfort and convenience of its members.[40]

Much, however, will be determined by the earth's potential carrying capacity and the technology by which it may be realized. Postponing for a few pages the problems of resources and ecological effects, let us view through the looking glass of the green revolution and survey just how many people this planet might be able to feed.

As long as man must rely on photosynthesis[41] as the process by which he produces his food, there is a limit to the supply potential. The plant is a biological food-making machine powered by the sun. It takes raw materials from various sources, processes them, and renders them fit to eat. Sometimes we eat the machine itself; sometimes we eat the creatures that have eaten the machine; but in every case, whether the food is vegetable, fish, livestock, or fowl, our nourishment derives from photosynthesis and ultimately the received energy of the solar disc.

The sun, we know, arrived on the scene long before our planet, about 6 billion years ago, as a natural nuclear explosion fusing atoms of hydrogen to form the slightly more complex element helium. When all its hydrogen is consumed, the light will go out, and all life dependent on the sun—which is the only form we are aware of—will come to an end. But we are assured that there is enough hydrogen remaining in the sun to fuel the process for another 8 billion years before our share of the energy received begins to drop off from what it is today.

The size of that share has long been accurately surveyed, and though it is only one five hundred millionth of the energy sphere formed by the sun radiating in every outward direction, it is immense indeed. When measured in calories, as is normally done, it comes to about 16,400 for every square yard of the earth's surface every minute of the year. In a single year the earth receives 1.25 billion trillion (1,250,000,000,000,000,000,000) calories of solar energy. What we call a calorie, it will be remembered, is the amount of heat needed to raise the temperature of a kilogram of water one degree Centigrade (actually, scientists call this a kilogram-calorie, but that need not concern us here). Not all of this energy is available for photosynthesis. Some 60 percent is in fact lost through reflection by the clouds and absorption in the atmosphere. Of the balance, about one-half lies in a region at the red end of the spectrum, which is useless to the photosynthetic process. Of what remains, some is dissipated by reflection from the oceans, the mountains, the deserts, the city streets, and the plant machine itself.

In the end, it has been calculated, the plant life we possess today takes in only 12 percent of the energy dispatched to us from the sun, and as a plant is a most inefficient machine, it presently makes use of only a fraction of that. Scientists have demonstrated that a plant, when it absorbs 320 calories of sunlight, can convert raw materials into 112 calories of organic matter. This is an efficiency rate of about 35 percent. Higher rates have been achieved under laboratory conditions, and the theoretical maximum, according to Niciporovic, is 75 percent, but in actual practice efficiency falls to some 3 percent. The plants fail to live up to their potential because of poorly fertilized soils, inadequate water supplies, and improper temperatures. Nevertheless, utilizing less than .4 percent of the amount of sunlight it takes in, our present plant machinery produces an enormous weight of vegetation, which has recently been estimated at about 400 billion tons each year. This is the quantity that theoretically can in one way or another be harvested annually without destroying any part of replenishment capacity.

But only a very tiny portion—not much more than .1 percent—of the 400 billion tons is consumed by human beings as plant food. Another, even smaller, portion is fed by us to animals so that we may later eat the eggs, milk products, and meat derived from them. Another minuscule amount goes to the fish we catch for food. Still another is taken or set aside by man for wood, fibers, and other purposes such as landscapes, parks, and floriculture. After all this, however, over 99 percent is left untouched, given over to wild animals, the birds, and every other living thing, from elephants to microbes. That that allotment is more than generous—though not always fairly apportioned—can be seen in the tremendous amount of organic growth that goes to waste each year, since most of it simply falls to the ground and rots.

All of this suggests three directions in which efforts to increase food supplies might proceed without much resistance. There is, first, a wide area into which plant efficiency might be expanded; second, the plant machinery itself might be enlarged by extending the land under cultivation; and third, one might harvest a greater portion of the annual gross plant product.

Today, especially since the appearance of the green revolution, a combination of all three methods is being carried out, and it seems likely that this trend will continue. We need only concern ourselves with the first and second methods, however, because the latter of the two—the extension of agriculture—implies a certain amount of encroachment on areas, notably in the tropics, that are already covered by plant growth whose product is inedible and presently goes to waste.

Regarding the first method, we have seen that the new technology in wheat, rice, and other grains has greatly increased plant efficiency, in many cases bringing it near its present-day potential of 35 percent. Although this, too, is capable of expansion, let us use the 35 percent rate as the standard we may achieve with existing technology. This alone would increase food supplies almost twelve times what it now is, and, in the process, it is fair to imagine, something would be done to eliminate much of the great spoilage suffered each year due to poor storage and marketing, currently estimated at more than 20 percent.[42] We should therefore be not too far off if we settle for a fifteen-fold increase in food supplies.

In connection with the second method, the FAO has calculated that on the basis of the green revolution the 3.5 billion acres now under crops throughout the world could be expanded to 15 billion acres, or to about the same extent Borlaug estimated in 1964. Of this figure, according to FAO's Walter Pawley, "not less than half would be in zones [the tropics] with growing temperatures around the year where three crops could be grown . . ."[43] That means that 7.5 billion acres could be cropped three times annually, which is the equivalent of 22.5 billion crop-acres (7.5 billion × 3), and the remainder, 7.5 billion acres in the temperate zones, would yield one crop a year, giving a total of 30 billion crop-acres. Since the world average intensity of cultivation, according to the FAO, is below one crop a year (perhaps three crops in four years),[44] we arrive at a figure considerably more than ten times the crop-acres presently harvested.

Now, if we combine the two multiples derived from an increase in efficiency and the extension of cultivated land, we are left with a factor of 150, with which we can calculate that the earth, with regard to food supplies, would not be coming up against the inner barrier of its carrying capacity until it had 150 times its present population—that is, 525 billion people. So wide is the door being opened by the green revolution.

Admittedly these are very rough estimates. They do not, for example, take into consideration the relationship between edible food produced and the entire growth achieved by photosynthesis, as well as the many variables that influence the photosynthetic function. This is a complex problem in geometry, involving such factors as average leaf size, the manner in which leaves are displayed, temperature, and the changing conditions of both the sky and the position of the sun, which in turn is dependent on the seasons and the latitude where a crop is grown.

The problem, however, has been worked out on a computer by a Dutch research scientist in photosynthesis, C. T. de Wit, who sought to determine the precise limits of the plant machine as a food provider.[45] De Wit considered as cultivable land all areas of the globe that have average daily temperatures of 50 degrees Fahrenheit for at least one full month of the year. This gave him a surface about *twice* as large as the one we have used above, and curiously enough, the conclusion printed out by the computer was that the earth's carrying capacity was about *double* our figure, or slightly more than 1 trillion people.

De Wit reported his findings at a scientific symposium held in Chicago in 1966. This was before the results of the green revolution could be foreseen, but his model had an advanced tropical technology built into it by the assumption that the means would be found to cultivate the tropics, which have an average temperature of more than 50 degrees Fahrenheit all year around, at the high performance rate already achieved in the Netherlands. Such means have now been demonstrated.

Thus it can be seen that demographic growth theoretically places absolutely no strain on our food-making capacity, since long before the world's population would approach the first limits of photosynthesis, it would arrive at a much more formidable obstacle: the limitations of space.

Although the glib extrapolators of the population explosion forecast that unless their recommendations are followed, the earth will contain 1 trillion people by the year 2250, our species, as we conceive of its existence on this planet, can never come close to that number. As de Wit and others have shown, in order to feed such a quantity of human beings almost all the planet's land surface would have to be given over to agriculture, and the people would have to live near the poles and at sea. Many years before such a foolhardy and needless decision might be contemplated, however, the population would have stabilized at some unknown level higher than it is today, if not by a culturally induced decline in growth rates, then by rising death rates brought on by whatever might be the minimum space required to support land-based human life. We may therefore discard the 1 trillion figure.

How great the stabilized population might be, as has been noted, is incalculable. Harrison Brown, a member of the Commission on the Year 2000, has projected a figure of 15 billion.[46] This would appear to be below the "proper and natural extent" of mankind, since the economies and synergistic benefits of high population densities probably could not be attained worldwide at such a level. In any event, Brown believes 15 billion to be the lowest possible figure achievable given the present momentum. Pawley, of the FAO, has suggested the late twenty-first century as "the earliest date by which a stationary population could be reached."[47] We would at that time, according to his computations, be left with a population of about 36 billion. Such numbers would give a world density that compares favorably with that of highly affluent regions, such as the coastal area between Boston and Washington, countries of the Common Market, and Japan. Whether this is the optimum, however, is debatable. It would seem wiser to prepare to accommodate a larger amount of people.

On the other hand, the 525 billion arrived at above

seems much too large for comfort. In a developed economy, it has been determined, men require, apart from the space occupied by their agriculture, at least 420 square yards per person for urban needs.[10] In addition, an equal measure is said to be required for recreation areas, such as parks, beaches, and landscape. This is undoubtedly a bit too optimistic. The region between Boston and Washington, an economically advanced zone with probably the highest standard of living in the world, has an urban population of about that degree, but anyone who has ever lived there, at least in its metropolitan areas, can offer testimony as to its space inadequacy. Some redistribution of population density would make these figures feasible, but a world population of 525 billion would demand urban-recreation areas nearly four times as dense as they are between Boston and Washington.

If, however, we allow for per-person urban-recreation needs not the recommended 840 square yards but 1,210 (which is exactly one-quarter of an acre), this might be considered a step forward, particularly by the city dwellers in the Boston–Washington zone, since it would have the effect of reducing the population density under which they live by almost 50 percent. It is one-fourth the present density of Los Angeles, one-twenty-fifth that of Calcutta, and one-thirtieth that of Manhattan, which has a population density of more than 77,000 persons per square mile.

Were the rather spacious per-person allotment of one-fourth acre for urban and recreation requirements to be the global average, the world's population would be approximately 108 billion people. For the sake of convenience, let us round the figure to an even 100 billion and risk the statement that such may be the dimensions of the giant in the earth.

An urban population density of a quarter-acre for every

man, woman, and child, that is, 2,560 persons per square mile, ought to satisfy the highest needs of the most claustrophobic town dweller. Hardly a city in America remains that roomy. Madison, Tucson, Tacoma, and San Diego would fall into the same general category of spaciousness, though all have a somewhat greater density. Seen another way, New York City, when slavery was abolished there on July 4, 1827, had a demographic distribution of about a quarter-acre per man, as had many of the great towns of Europe of the late Middle Ages and the Renaissance. If today a population density of this measure implies a radical redistribution of people, then here is still another of the unignorable dilemmas created by the population imperative with which the social system must deal. As the established order cannot, because of arbitrarily fixed state boundaries, manage the problem peacefully, it does not even recognize it as yet—a most dangerous form of blindness. But were it handled rationally, we could look forward, for one thing, to a decline in petty, divisive nationalism, an artifice of a certain historic period, which continues to be the cause of much bloodshed and human suffering.

What sort of diet would the giant have?

There appears to be little reason to indulge in the activity of counting calories and weighing proteins. Nutritionists have yet to agree on how many calories a man needs,[49] and still less precise is their knowledge of protein requirements. Science for many years has had to engage itself in an arduous labor of deflating the false claims of dietitians, fund-raisers, book merchants, food packagers, milk salesmen, and all manner of special interest groups as to what the content of our daily fare should be. Calorie and protein requirements were more than once shown to have been overestimated. Weight-to-height ratios have been substantially lowered, for reasons of health, as have been an imagined vital need for eggs, butter, milk, meat, and animal fats. Nutrition scientists, such as Nevin Scrimshaw, have demonstrated that it is simply pure fiction that one must eat animal food to obtain protein needs (the dwarf wheats contain 12 percent protein). Worse is the uncritical acceptance of a widely sloganed "protein gap" in the underdeveloped countries,[50] since on analysis deficiencies may be seen to be linked not to food supplies but to poverty both in the underdeveloped and in the developed world. Worse still is the racist-originated notion that such deficiencies lead to impaired mental ability in human beings, which adversely affect their intelligence.[51] This carries with it the implication that the millions of undernourished people now alive in the Third World are our structural inferiors for whom not a thing can be done.

This persistent idea, favored by many neo-Malthusian population controllers, is wholly unproved. An example of how widely and how harmfully it has spread may be seen in the unwitting statement made by the director of West Bengal's health services, who disclosed in July, 1971, that 300,000 refugee children from Bangladesh were near starvation. "Even if we save many children's lives," he was reported as having declared, "those under four years old may already have suffered permanent, irreversible brain damage."[52] So why bother to save them, more than a few people may have concluded, particularly since there are "too many Asians" anyway? The truth is, however, that no responsible scientist can infer a causal relationship between poor nutrition and impaired mental ability, though many have shown poor social conditions to be a major culprit.[53]

According to an FAO document on a recent symposium of well-known nutrition scientists from the United States and Europe:

> All scientists who attended the Symposium and who had worked on this problem agreed that great caution should be exercised in drawing conclusions as to the final effect of malnutrition on behavior and mental development. There is as yet no definite basis for concluding that the changes described in the brain of malnourished animals and children are the cause of changes of behavior and of impairment of functions.[54]

That not enough is known about the effects of protein deficiency on the brain is strikingly illustrated by the work of an Indian researcher who reported his findings at an international conference held at Cambridge, Massachusetts, a few years ago.[55] His experiments in an Indian orphanage showed that children who were receiving high-protein dietary supplements had *lower* mental-age scores than a control group who were not getting the extra protein.

Finally, Scrimshaw, one of the world's most eminent nutritionists, and his colleague John E. Gordon, have stated, in a recent book entitled *Malnutrition, Learning, and Behavior*, that it is "crystal clear" that to show poor nutrition to be a cause of low intelligence, "it is necessary to demonstrate an effect distinct from that caused by social conditions . . . the informed opinion [is] that this is yet to be done." [56]

Leaving protein and calorie counting aside, it seems clear enough that if, as we have earlier seen, an expansion of the world's crop-acreage to 30 billion was theoretically sufficient, under high-level agriculture, to support a population of 525 billion, we may now, for a population of 100 billion, cut back the crop-acreage figure five and a quarter times. This leaves a requirement of about 5.7 billion crop-acres for the food and forestry-product needs of such a population.

Since the world's land area, excluding Antarctica, is 32 billion acres, and 25 billion would have to be given over to urban-recreation areas, we are left with 7 billion for agricultural use. Depending upon where on the globe these lands are situated, they can give us a crop-acreage figure of anywhere from below 7 billion (less than one crop a year) to above 21 billion (more than three crops a year). Thus if only 5.7 billion crop-acres are actually needed and in excess of 21 billion are available, not to mention all foods from the sea, our giant would have considerable freedom to select any diet he might fancy.

Even the gloomiest demographers cannot foresee a world of 100 billion people until sometime in the second quarter of the twenty-second century. We are therefore entitled, by the experience of history, to assume that a number of technological advances will take place in the interim, which will enhance the capacity described above to cater to the food needs (and whims) of the 100 billion. We may learn to peel away the cloud cover over agricultural lands to increase the quantity of light available for photosynthesis. Or, what amounts to the same thing, we may decide, as has already been done experimentally, to illuminate our fields at night with high-energy laser beams.[57] Or, we may do both, and apply various other food-related technologies now being given a try and those still to come. All would tend to reduce crop-acreage, and so free more and more areas for less functional, pleasurable uses. In the United States, for example, advances in agricultural technology have permitted a 20 percent reduction of farm acreage between 1930 and 1970. In the absence of such progress, says agronomist Keith Barrons, U.S. population growth would have required a 100 percent *increase* in croplands to feed the present number of Americans. Thus, Barrons adds, "for each acre tilled today another acre is available for optional uses . . ." —releasing from exploitation land amounting to 290 million acres.[58]

If we examine the innovations that took place during the same time span as we are dealing with prior to the landing on the moon, taking us back to the last days of George Washington; if we study—as Toffler has done in *Future Shock*—the rate of acceleration of technology, which has reached the point at which 90 percent of all scientists who ever lived are alive today,[59] the relative impotence of imagination is pitifully unmasked. It takes no imagination, however, to realize that to support 100 billion people at present, albeit inadequate, world standards the annual increase in agricultural output over the next 150 to 175 years need only be about 2 percent. By way of comparison, from 1952 to 1969, before the impact of the green revolution, agricultural production in the seventy-five underdeveloped countries classified as such by the FAO grew at an average of 2.9 percent a year or almost 50 percent more than the low-standard requirement.[60] Since 1969 in the poor countries of south and southeast Asia, where the new technology has made the farthest inroads, agriculture has been growing at 4 percent annually.[61] Food production in 1970 increased 5 percent over the year before, and the average for the underdeveloped countries as a whole (in Asia, Africa, and Latin America) was 4 percent.[62] In the underdeveloped countries, according to FAO projections, agricultural production during the decade 1970–80 is expected to grow at 3.3 percent a year—a rate 15 percent higher than that of the previous decade.[63] In other words, irrigation, fertilizer use, and all the other technologies needed to maximize agricultural productivity, as well as the necessary capital investment, must expand over the period at 2 percent per year—much below the current rate—to achieve the thirtyfold rise in production as the minimum need of the projected population. Borlaug's retracted statement of 1964 that the green revolution could feed the world for the next two centuries would appear to have been right after all. Pawley, however, has shown, as we have seen, that a *fiftyfold* increase was a "distinct possibility" in less than 100 years, which is why he has concluded that it is "a fundamental mistake to link the population question primarily to food supplies."[64]

Thus the pressure the population explosion is applying to the social system, making it hurt so badly and so loudly, causing so much pain and worry, comes not from fear that the food needs of the giant in the earth can be met. In reality, the pressure emerges from the corollary prospect that the long-term 2 percent rate, or something like it, is also the pace at which land tenure, income distribution, industry, resources, energy, and all the laws, fast-talk, and sleights-of-hand that keep off the have-nots from the haves, must be shifted in favor of the have-nots. This would signify a complete reversal of the historic trend.

At the end of the eighteenth century the distance between the poorest countries of the world and the richest, if measured by the ratio of per-capita incomes in southern India and Great Britain, was 1:8.[65] In 1971, with the center of wealth moved to the United States, the difference between the poorest nations' and the American average was 1:60, and if the present trend were to continue, before the end of the century, it would be 1:100. Relatively speaking, the poor would then be 12½ times poorer than they were in the late 1700s and, seen from the perspective of population, they would outnumber the rich countries not 2½ times, as they do today, but by ten to one.

Somewhere on this mangy camel's back the last straw may fall. René Dumont and Bernard Rosier have hazarded the guess that long before the century's end the gulf between the wastefully overconsuming rich and the deprived poor "will provoke violent reprisals which may even destroy our civilization."[66] Pawley sees the "breaking point" as imminent. There are "already," he has written, major political units where the whole economic and social structure is on the verge of collapse as a result of this kind of pressure. "The danger that the whole social system may break down for hundreds of millions of people is a real one," he says.[67]

Arguments like these, usually advanced to promote population control as the primary therapy for the world's ills, are of the scare variety and are much overdrawn. They appeal to the conservation of rather questionable values, cherished most highly by minority elites. Civilizations, such as they are, rarely "collapse," and much less are they destroyed; they are transformed, and more often simply attuned to changing times—if with hardship for all concerned. Secondly, the poor, unfortunately, have shown an astonishing capacity to suffer increasingly greater burdens, bartering ever-larger portions of sweat and human dignity in exchange for the jealously guarded, meagerly apportioned right to live. But even the poor have limited means (this, too, history reveals), and though no one can tell which straw is the last, it cannot on a historic time scale be very far from hand.

In any event the changes that must ensue from the population imperative will not be caused by a substantive inability to produce enough food, wood, and fiber. Whether the ecological effects of the green revolution technologies and a future rapidly building up to 100 billion people will be tolerated by the environment as a whole, however, is another matter, which ought to be carefully explored.

III

ECOLOGY FEVER

THE SAME PEOPLE who publicize their own and others' private nightmares about the plow's being unable to keep up with the stork are to be found on the other side of the population equation: that of pollution riding hard by the wheels of the pram.[1]

That this is evidently false may be made clear by the statement of a few simple facts.

India's population is growing three times as fast as America's; it has twice as many people and a density ten times as large. Yet India contributes very little pollution to the biosphere, while America contributes more than any other country.

Sydney, Australia, has air- and water-pollution problems, even though the total population of that continent, which is 80 percent as large as the United States, is only 6 percent of America's.

Moreover, in the heartland of the ecology "crisis" itself, great armies of researchers looking hard have gathered little data to support the notion of a significant relationship between population growth and environmental pollution. On the contrary, as ecologist Barry Commoner and the director of Princeton University's population research office, Ansley Coale, have shown, economic factors are far more important than demographic growth as an environmental threat. Commoner says flatly that population growth in the United States can in "no way" account for the rapid increase in pollution levels since 1946. He suggests that the principal cause is the economic system we live under. Thus in the postwar period from 1946 to 1966, while fertilizer use in the United States went up 700 percent, pesticide 500 percent, electric power 400 percent, and fuel consumption 100 percent, population in the United States increased only 43 percent.[2] For those who feel more crowded than that last figure might suggest, one of the reasons is implicit in the fact that while the population in America has grown since 1940 by 50 percent, attendance at national parks, for example, has gone up by more than 400 percent.[3]

It is true that the ecological effects of the green revolution, emerging from the impact of demographic pressure, though often inflated, are nevertheless real. From our point of view, these effects may be said to range widely indeed: from whatever risks may be involved in tampering with plant evolution to the likely outcome of the resource demands of a much larger population than exists today. There are also, as will be seen below, important environmental *benefits* derived from the green revolution.

Nevertheless the new technologies are, for example, going to increase the amount of chemical residues running into the seas from fertilizers and pesticides, although at rates not nearly approaching the 1946–66 figures. The answers to these particular problems may have to come from the biological control of pests, for which the future offers "many exciting possibilities," to use the words of F. J. Simmonds, a specialist reporting to the Royal Society in 1970,[4] and from such techniques as cell fusion, which permits the endowment of some plants with the ability of others to fertilize themselves naturally. In this connection, a Rand Corporation study has forecast that crop characteristics will be interchangeable through genetic engineering probably within the next two decades.[5]

Certainly global birth control is not a solution, if only because the most effective method proposed is the massive introduction into the environment of the loathed offender itself: dangerous chemicals, in the form of the pill and other contraceptive drugs. As James Ridgeway has pointed out, "Just as pesticides can break down the environment by killing fish and aquatic plants, so can birth-control instruments break down the environment by causing harmful physical and psychological effects in women." [6]

All who yearn for the fail-safe pill might more wisely give the right-of-way to an improved fertilizer and pesticide technology. High-speed population growth must one day grind to a halt, but there can be no foreseeable return to archaic agriculture.

The establishment of priorities, however, will remain impossible as long as the problems of the green revolution are used to fan the hysteria that accompanies ecology fever, an hallucinatory malady caused perhaps by the shock of the population explosion. It is a futile exercise to attempt to answer all the criticisms of those whose temperature has been elevated by that ailment. The *idée fixe* about a population bomb, and the death-oriented, life-negating means by which it is to be defused, raise doubts about the flexibility of such men and their movements to address themselves seriously to the matters involved.

Kenneth Boulding, who believes in a world population "toward" 100 million [7] (what is to become of the remaining 3,400,000,000 of us?) lends support to such movements, although his reluctance to take himself and his colleagues seriously is to be admired. In a candid lecture given at Yale University in 1969, under the auspices of the Ford Foundation, Boulding, who thinks the economic development of the poor countries will result in the "final catastrophe," gave the following report on a meeting in which he participated:

> An extraordinary conference was held last December [1968] . . . It was an antidevelopment gathering of ecologists, who presented sixty developmental horror stories, among them predictions that the Aswan Dam is going to ruin Egypt, the Kariba Dam will ruin central Africa, DDT will ruin us all, insecticides will ruin the cotton crops, thallium will ruin Israel, and so on all down the line. Some of these forecasts I take with a little grain of ecological salt. The cumulative effect, however, is significant, and suggests that no engineer should be allowed into the world without an ecologist in attendance as a priest.[8]

This would be rather amusing, were it not that men like Boulding, and the "horror stories" of ecology fever and the population explosion, exercise a powerful influence on American foreign and domestic policy to the benefit of a few and the inconvenience of multitudes. What is needed, rather than lighthearted views about the possible exaggerations of ecologists self-styled or otherwise, is a penetrating look at the movements, which boast that their time has come and which have so captured the public's attention. It is not possible to examine the long- and short-term implications of the green revolution, when at every turn we are greeted with jeers of "ruin, ruin, ruin." Previously we sought to demonstrate that the neo-Malthusian view had the food-population axis on its head; now it may be useful to show that the entire phenomenon is looking backward.

Leading population-explosionist Paul Ehrlich, in one of those Yale-Ford Foundation lectures, said frankly that, "It is quite clear that a lot of people who advocate population control really mean to stop the blacks from breeding . . ."[9] But such people are simply racists, said Ehrlich, who admits to hoping that the Third World "stays underdeveloped,"[10] and who believes that the chances of Indians' learning how to use fertilizer on their crops correctly "seems to be about zero."[11]

We have the words of the protagonists themselves to tell us more about them. The "ultimate catastrophe" for Ehrlich was the "disastrous decline in the death rate" in the poor countries as a result of "our" medical technology, as well as a rise in the birth rates "thanks to the eradication of such diseases as gonorrhea in areas where it causes a certain amount of sterility."[12] Such is Ehrlich's unhappiness. Boulding, who sometimes writes in verse, feels the development of the poor countries to be an "evil" thing.

He sings:

> With development extended to the whole of
> planet earth
> What started with abundance may conclude in
> dismal dearth.[13]

But he is not really worried because the "presently underdeveloped countries are not going to develop." This is not the result of a system of past and present exploitation, he says; he explains it this way: "If some countries are rich and some are poor, it is because the rich countries are on the main line of development . . . The reason for the United States' wealth today is that we have had fairly consistent economic growth for well over 150 years." [14] Why? Because it is.

It is most instructive to learn the opinions of the director of the program on social and economic dynamics at the University of Colorado's Institute of Behavioral Science (Professor Boulding) and the chairman of Zero Population Growth, Inc. (Professor Ehrlich). But this is far from the searching analysis we so require. Fortunately, this job has been done, most thoroughly by a team of sociologists, William Barclay, Joseph Enright, and Reid T. Reynolds, in their investigative report, *Population Control in the Third World* (published in 1970), and by James Ridgeway, in his book, *The Politics of Ecology* (1970).

Both studies trace the ecology and population-control movements back to a well-known handful of white supremacists, and later to powerful conservative and reactionary interests, whose primary aim is to secure unchallengeable access to the world's resources necessary to maintain established society in the United States.

It is only natural that a nation that has but 6 percent of the world's population and accounts for 50 to 60 percent of the annual consumption of the world's nonrenewable resources [15] should express concern about demographic and developmental pressure on the mountains of its wealth. But, of course, the problem could hardly be articulated publicly in quite those terms, particularly by those who have the most to conserve—which is why the movements got under way.

The documentation presented by the Barclay group is

impressive. It discerns an indisputable "population establishment," a compact, interlocking power structure [16] tied primarily to the most profound interests of the Fords, the Rockefellers, the Mellons, Carnegie, General Motors, and Du Pont. The names of the policy-makers and financial backers of such American organizations as the Population Council, the Population Reference Bureau, Planned Parenthood, Population Crisis Committee, and the Campaign to Check the Population Explosion read like a *Who's Who* of the most powerful and influential people in the world.

The team's critique, which represents a qualitative expansion of a paper presented in 1970 at a meeting of the Population Association of America, shows how private wealth was used to create a public and governmental commitment to the interests of private wealth.

"At the time we started work [1952]," John D. Rockefeller III said in 1969, "any government participation [in population control] would have been politically unthinkable." [17]

According to the Barclay-Enright-Reynolds study:

> While John D. Rockefeller III was moving into the population control business, his brother Laurence . . . served on the U.S. President's Materials Policy Commission, which began its 1952 report by asking whether or not the United States had the raw materials necessary to "sustain its civilization." . . . [It] concluded that the United States had the necessary resources—but only if we could rely on Third World supplies. [The report includes] numerous tables and projections concerning U.S. economic dependence on foreign sources of raw materials, and warns that population growth in Third World countries "presses hard on available natural resources."

Just as, according to Malthus, the poor were going

> to devour all the food, so now the poor throughout the world threaten the prodigious consumption of raw materials by the "developed" capitalist world. . . . By the 1970s of course, it was taken for granted by all concerned that the growing population of the Third World threatened the resource base of the world. Thus, Secretary of Commerce Maurice Stans could announce that one of the prime concerns of a new commission on raw materials would be the "unprecedented premium" that the world's rapid population growth places "on the limited resources of this planet." [18]

During the twenty-year period in which the "unthinkable" came to be "taken for granted," the population establishment undertook the costly labor of creating a popular base for its activities. Through a system of program grants to leading universities, and training and travel awards to individual scholars, particularly in demography, ecology, and associated fields, it built a constituency in the academic world. As there is nothing many scholars like better than a grant and a free trip abroad, a pressure group was created among "objective" social scientists, who have a strong voice in Washington, a way with the press, and the confidence of the public.

Between 1952 and 1968 the Ford Foundation, for example, spent almost $30 million for these purposes. More than one-third of this amount went for the establishment of a dozen university centers "focusing on population problems." [19] Many of the individuals and institutions who received these grants provided the personnel, influence, and philosophy that finally involved American public funds in population control to the extent of $100 million a year. In 1971 Ford reported: "Since government and international agencies are now enlarging their role in the population field—mainly by funding action programs—the Foundation's commitments no longer exceed those from all other private and public funding sources, as they did for nearly two decades."[20]

It was in the second of those two decades—the infamous sixties—that the interests of the population controllers rapidly began to fall side by side with those concerned with conservation, ecology, pollution, "the crime explosion," and the uppityness of nonwhite people at home and abroad. It was not possible to form a coalition of groups; nor was this desired. Instead a hundred flowers were allowed to bloom, which is why the movement was able to broaden its appeal to include old-time racists, the corporate elite, rising politicians, well-meaning liberals, and student radicals. What was achieved in the process was the neo-Malthusian consensus, with its prevailing reductionist view that all the world's ills are caused by not enough contraception, and that the end result of this failing was breaking down our ecosystem.

The neo-Malthusian consensus, the triumph of the Ford and Rockefeller foundations, first emerged as a dominant force between 1968 and 1970. This was publicly expressed in a series of advertisements in *The New York Times,* signed by what the Barclay group calls "a brilliant cross-section of our ruling class with a few of the best brains money can buy thrown in for window dressing."[21] More important, further analysis of the ninety-four signers of the ads reveals a line that transcends the immediate issues and runs into the governmental and international institutions—such as AID, the United Nations, and, above all, the World Bank—which exercise a high level of control over the manner in which the poor countries are attempting to develop their societies (see Chapter VII).

These consensus ads brought up a plurality of issues and a single solution: population control, by one means or another. There was no problem under the sun that could not in this way be resolved, and indeed, in the end, the slogan would be: "Whatever your cause, it's a lost cause, without population control."

Among the problems touched on in the ads were the old standbys: famine and the Communist threat: "A world with mass starvation in underdeveloped countries," went one appeal, "will be a world of chaos, riots, and war. And a perfect breeding ground for Communism. . . . Our own national interest demands that we go all out to help the underdeveloped countries control their populations."

Raising fears of a foreign nonwhite peril became another theme: "The ever mounting tidal wave of humanity now challenges us to control it, or be submerged along with all our civilized values." Another ad brings the threat nearer: "Youngsters account for almost half the crimes. And in a few short years millions more of them will pour into the streets at the present rate of procreation. . . . Birth control tackles the problem at its source."

Finally, ecology: "Warning: The water you're drinking may be polluted." The reason for this is not industrial wastes carelessly dumped in the rivers; nor is it defective sewerage resulting from political corruption, bribery, and kickbacks. The "*basic cause,*" says the ad in words underlined, is "the rising flood of humanity abroad," and, since Americans are in a better position to object to being called a human flood, "the rising population of the United States."

James Ridgeway, commenting on this particular advertisement, wrote at the time:

> The neo-Malthusian doctrine which now is emerging from the ecologists among the conservation groups

and the technocrats at the World Bank looks pretty much like a narrow manipulative scheme for advancing the interests of the U.S. industrialists. In this instance, the "New Class" scientists/technocrats are joined by the old-fashioned property owning elites. . . . Now they talk about population control. This is aimed at the poor. But it's not the poor who exploited the resources of this continent and turned the waterways into open sewers. . . . The signers of *The New York Times* ad include George Champion of the Chase Manhattan Bank (Rockefeller); Frank W. Abrams, of Standard Oil of New Jersey [Rockefeller]; Lamont du Pont Copeland of du Pont; David E. Lilienthal, TVA; and Mrs. Cordelia Scaife May of the Mellon clan. The ad was paid for by Hugh Moore, founder of Dixie Cup [who also paid for the promotion of Ehrlich's *The Population Bomb* [23]]. Oil, coal, chemicals, paper —the industries which have fouled the continent from one end to another. Their representatives now ask that the masses control the size of their families so that the plunder can continue.* [24]

Then came Earth Day. Ridgeway sums it up well in his book:

> Ecology touched millions of ordinary white middle class people as no other political issue had for years. It aroused smouldering passions for a pre-industrial past, reviving the tradition of American individualism, of man in nature. . . .
>
> But the protestations of a President, the celebrations of Earth Day, a crusade by students with their arms full of non-returnable bottles . . . [merely] pro-

* In this connection, the United States in 1971 for the first time began financing human sterilization domestically—starting in the depressed Appalachian hill country. In a pilot project marking a change in long-standing policy, the Office of Economic Opportunity allocated a quarter of a million dollars to promote and pay for sterilization surgery for volunteers among the 30,000 isolated and poor people of Anderson County, Tennessee.

> vided a cover behind which the ecology interests could wage their struggle for control of natural resources . . . the underground war for control of water-pollution programs, the key to control of other environmental policies, and the battle among the petroleum trusts for domination of the world energy markets.[25]

The ecologists, Ridgeway perceives, are the rhetoricians who talk in radical terms about the "quality of life" and reorganizing society, but function as a screen for corporate interests, particularly the petroleum industry. The burning of fossil fuels in the United States creates most of the world's pollution (the American production-consumption pattern makes for much of the balance), and Ridgeway has shown that the biggest polluters are the biggest supporters of the antipollution crusade. "These large corporations," he explains, "anticipate that by dominating the ecology movement, they can influence the rate and manner in which pollution control is achieved."[26]

All this does not suggest some dark conspiracy of wicked men trying to hoodwink the people. It ought to be remembered that some pollution control is better than none, and that Ford and Rockefeller were the fundamental underwriters of the green revolution both vaunted and disparaged by their allies and themselves. History knows many families and institutions that have founded their successes on being all things to all men. It does suggest, however, that one must take with more than "a grain of ecological salt" all the claims of ruin signed and countersigned by dependent men.

Reading any fair sample of the voluminous literature on the ecological "crisis," one is bound to be struck by how the known damage—as sorrowful as it is—fails to live up to the fears expressed, and that the extent of what is actually known is very limited. The serious literature on the subject is covered with phrases such as "it is extremely difficult to prove . . ."; "we do not really know . . ."; and "there are some signs of . . ." [27] Ansley Coale, speaking of the deterioration of our environment and the population explosion, has wisely cautioned that "there is no valid reason for hasty action." [28]

Yet blood-curdling scenarios of doomsday-just-around-the-corner proliferate. Thirty-three British scientists lend their name to a "blueprint for survival," which if it were not insidiously reactionary would merely—in the words of other scientists—"echo the old vague but self-congratulatory sentiments of the Puritans." [29] Sir Philip Baxter, on retiring as chairman of the Australian Atomic Energy Commission, asserts that the End is probably two decades away. And when it comes, he says, billions of people will be killed and "refugees of all sorts will stream toward Australia. . . . You've got to just batter them off, keep them away and look after your own survival." [30] Of course, Australia should thus consider bacteriological, chemical, and nuclear warfare, "and anything else that will enable one man to hold off a hundred." In warning Australia of its near destiny, Sir Philip has done a "useful job," says Sir Macfarlane Burnet.

Perhaps the most publicized work in the growing body of neoeschatological literature is *The Limits to Growth,* published in 1972. This somber document was prepared by Dennis L. Meadows, his team of researchers, and the computers of the Massachusetts Institute of Technology. It represents the first pronouncement of an organization known as the Club of Rome set up four years ago mainly by industrialists to study the "predicament of mankind."

The report, which cost the Volkswagen Foundation a quarter of a million dollars to produce, forecasts global collapse and nothing but collapse "within the next one hundred years."[31] There is only one way to avoid this: by creating an everlasting state of equilibrium, "with benefits for all," and founded on a "basic change of values and goals at individual, national and world levels." The leaders of the New Society would be, at least in the first stage, "the economically developed countries."[32]

The Limits to Growth, a simplification of the naïve works of Jay W. Forrester,[33] is more Malthus than Malthus. Whereas the Master had no illusions about the ineluctable character of exponential growth, his pessimism being complete, the Club of Rome, while "unequivocally"[34] denying any intention of wishing to freeze the status quo, raises the evangelical banner: "Repent, or the end of the world is at hand!"

The scientific journal *Nature,* commenting on the MIT study, asks: "So how does it come about that Malthus's prediction of disaster for the British population . . . failed to pass?" It offers an answer:

> Dr. Meadows and his colleagues would have had a more convincing tale to tell if they had been seen to be more aware of where their predecessors went astray. And the truth is, of course, that the British population, like the population of the rest of Western Europe and North America, has in the past century and a half (but only just) gone through a period of historic change in which a reduction of death rate, often but not always the mainspring of population increase, has been followed by a reduction of birth rate and by a demographic condition which, taking one decade with another, can only be called stability. . . .
>
> The truth, which those who manipulate exponential growth curves seem consistently to overlook, is that there is nothing in the history of the past century to

> suggest that developing countries are intrinsically less capable than were developed countries of striking a sensible demographic balance, that many developing communities seem to be within a generation of such a happy state but that it is in everybody's interest that the laggards should quickly follow suit. In short, the problem of world population is not a simple problem in the exponential calculus but a complicated aspect of the evolution of society. And there is practical experience to show that in the encouragement of lower birth rates in the developing world, utterances from the Club of Rome may be less effective than humane steps to reduce the prevalence of infant mortality.[35]

Projections based on what is happening in the present—any present—will invariably lead to doomsday or collapse. Every time period is beleaguered by problems which, if left unsolved, would bring on disaster. That is why they are always "solved," or rather more often shelved, postponed, transformed, forgotten, or discovered not to have been a problem at all. The nature of exponential growth foreordains the outcome of any projection. Doomsday is built in. A single bacterial cell can divide every twenty minutes—one becoming two, two four, four eight, and so on. This is exponential growth, and, in this case, were it to continue unimpeded, one such cell would, *in a single day,* produce a biomass equal to the size of and weight of this planet; an hour later it would be eight times as large. That this does not and cannot happen is governed by other mathematical laws of equal integrity. One does not have to know very much about differential calculus to understand that exponential growth must always give way to a less dramatic condition. Only in Wonderland or Oz can man and the creatures he knows violate the physical laws of the universe. Whoever gazes into the crystal ball of exponential growth to view the fate of the problems that today beset mankind must either project similar growth for his problem-solving capabilities or recite the tired story, already hoary when told in the Book of Daniel, of the Last Days of Man.

Much is left unsaid when prophets speak of doom. All those who categorically damn DDT—and have no desire to see human death rates climb—need to be reminded that DDT saved the lives of the 500 million persons who, according to Philip Handler of the National Academy of Sciences, "would inevitably have been the victims of malaria." [36] The World Health Organization has made the following statement:

> The safety record of DDT to man is truly remarkable. At the height of its production 400,000 tons a year were used for agriculture, forestry, public health, etc. Yet in spite of prolonged exposure by hundreds of millions of people, and the heavy occupational exposure of considerable numbers, the only confirmed cases of injury have been the result of massive accidental or suicidal swallowing of DDT. There is no evidence in man that DDT is causing cancer or genetic change.[37]

Pesticides of DDT variety have nothing in common with manna, but they are hardly the blot on the environment they are made out to be. The British Royal Commission on Environmental Pollution has said flatly that "there is no evidence that this [DDT] buildup constitutes any threat to human health." [38] And the American weekly *Science*, in a recent blast against "heavy-handed, opportunistic" ecologists, reported that a "sane toxicological evaluation" of suspected pollutants found *no pesticides of any kind* hazardous to humans.[39] There is still no medically documented case of ill health in man attributable to the proper use of pesticides, and, in contradiction to the familiar argument of biological accumulation, Soviet scientists have found that DDT can be broken down by microorganisms in the soil within a few months.[40] This challenges the widely held view that the substance's residues can degrade only over many years and therefore build up in man by way of the food chain. Moreover, it is not true that in passing through the food chain, insecticide concentration always increases. Recent studies have shown that in some instances deconcentration occurs, and it is a rarely mentioned fact that as the human body not only takes in but excretes DDT, an innocuous steady state is reached where the total trace amounts in the tissues remain constant.[41]

Although it is sound to be wary of all manner of pollution, the silent spring is not upon us, and it was Rachel Carson herself who said in 1962: "It is not my contention that chemical insecticides must never be used. . . . I am saying, rather, that control must be geared to realities, not to mythical situations . . ."[42] Somehow, since then, many myths have overtaken the realities.

Who, for example, would not now, in view of the hysteria, be surprised to learn, or relearn, as the case may be, that the urban areas of the United States occupy only *1 percent* of the entire land surface of the country?[43] That all the cursed freeways, highways, turnpikes, cloverleafs, backroads, and service roads; all the airports big and small, and the 200,000 miles of railroad tracks take up but another 1 percent, or a fraction more?[44] That the growth of our forests, which along with pastureland cover considerably more than half of America's land area, exceeds the total amount of annual tree removal by 60 percent?[45]

It is true that most man-made air pollution is a result of the combustion of fossil fuels, but most of the excess carbon dioxide, turpines, and other volatiles in the atmosphere come not from automobiles, smokestacks, and jet contrails but from decaying plant growth, rotting on soils that could be put to better use by man.[46] On the other hand, this is no excuse for the sulfur and lead being pumped into the skies by industry, or the wastes with which men foul the seas. Yet, the National Academy of Sciences reported in 1971 that "the average lead content of the air over most major cities apparently has not changed greatly over the last fifteen years," and "there is no evidence that the amount of lead in the diets of people has changed substantially since 1940." * [47] In the case of airborne sulfur, when it settles to the ground, it helps fertilize the soil,[48] and there are many places in the world (for example, Great Britain) where there is not enough sulfur in the soil and in the air. Further, there are organisms that thrive on marine pollution, bacteria that can feed on oil spills converting hydrocarbons into vivifying nutrients that enrich rather than spoil the sea.[49] Little research is being done on such bacteria, even less on how to move the sulfur in the air to where it may serve rather than do harm.

The polluted waterways are not dead; their waste-assimilative capacities have simply been overtried by too ambitious cost-benefit systems. They can recover, if men scale down the things they throw away. A recent United Nations study found that radioactive wastes are now being managed well, and that this form of marine pollution, at least, is expected to decline in spite of a projected sharp

* In a related development, a team of researchers in 1971 reported to the American Public Health Association that in spite of "ignorance and emotion," mercury in the environment and in human tissue had decreased sharply over the past sixty years, and that it does not present a health hazard. These findings were based on studies qualified by the pathologists involved as "the most extensive human-tissue study of mercury anywhere in the world."

increase in the number of nuclear reactors.[50] A device was reported that can isolate an oil slick and slowly drink it from the surface of the sea.

Ruined land can be reclaimed, water tables raised (or lowered). We can make rain. Soil erosion is preventable. What is needed is a deescalation not of human numbers but of human greed.

Although it is often overlooked by those who are eager to find ill only, the green revolution is highly beneficial to the environment in several ways. Apart from the ability of high-efficiency agriculture to release farmlands for other uses, the green revolution tends to protect and enrich the soils in which it grows. It contributes to erosion control, makes more effective use of water resources, retards the rate of residue runoff, and, as a consequence, the rate of water pollution. American agronomist Keith Barrons, in a monograph entitled "Environmental Benefits of Intensive Crop Production," explains:

> Today's high yields are equated with close plant spacing and vigorous growth. More unharvested portions of crop plants including roots are left in and on the soil when yields are high. These heavier crop residues contribute to an improved physical condition of the soil, better rainfall penetration and reduced erosion. . . . Intensive cropping with close stands and quick succession of one crop following another as now being practiced tend to minimize fertilizer losses to ground water or streams . . .

The unharvested stubble of the new dwarf varieties, he says, decompose and are incorporated into the soil, thus increasing its fertility, more readily than the plants they replaced.

A Giant in the Earth

To the many admonitions that our planet's resourcefulness is waning fast, there is much one can oppose.

As for minerals, a cubic mile of representative rock contains 1 billion tons of aluminum, 625 million tons of iron, 260 million tons of magnesium, and so on down to 60 tons of gold.[51] Indeed many specialists question the very validity of the term "nonrenewable resources." Coale writes:

> When we think of our resources of such useful materials as the metallic elements of iron, copper, nickel, lead, and so forth, we should realize that spaceship Earth has the same amount of each element as it had a million years ago, and will have the same amount a million years from now. All we do with these resources is to move them around. The energy we use is lost, but the minerals we find useful are still with us.[52]

And they are so abundant, he says, it does not pay to recycle them. He notes: "The price of raw materials relative to the price of finished goods is no higher now than at the beginning of the century, and if we were running out of raw materials, they would surely be rising in relative expensiveness."[53]

As Hans Landsberg, of Resources for the Future, has pointed out, the assumption that the population explosion in the underdeveloped countries threatens resource shortages is "shaky."

> Per capita income in most poor countries [he says] is so low that it will not for a long time to come support rising material consumption to a degree that will seriously eat into the world's resources. . . . And when in the much longer run some of these demands should arise, why assume that [say] steel will be the preferred material—just because in the nineteenth and the first

half of the twentieth centuries the Western world had nothing better to work with? Would it not be more reasonable to expect that developing countries will take off from where we *are* rather than where we *have been?*"[54]

What are resources for one generation are not necessarily those for another. Aluminum was once a jeweler's curiosity; iron ore was of no use to neolithic man. Further, it is an established economic fact that the advance of technology has on the average permitted the doubling of output from the same resource inputs every 35 years. Resources are a function of knowledge, research, and capital investment, not something to be measured in acres and tons. They are created by man from all that surrounds him, as a sculptor makes art out of stone.

Oddly enough, the problem in the poor countries, with regard to energy resources, is not overpopulation but, as in the case of the use of nuclear reactors, per-capita consumption and *user density*, according to Landsberg, "are too low to permit efficient use of such reactors."[55] Only in the more populated future can the Third World expect to derive these gains.

Most of the world's land-based resources (not to mention those in the sea, on the moon, and beyond) will abound for thousands of years more even at current wasteful, highly inefficient standards. The only one that appears to be in jeopardy is petroleum, although a commercially feasible process has been announced for the conversion into crude oil of manure, sewage, household garbage, and any organic waste products.[56] But if petroleum goes, good riddance. That it can be replaced by other, infinitely cleaner, means is beyond all doubt. Pollution-free generation of cheap electricity by tapping the heat radiating from the earth's core is already a reality in Italy and other countries, and it offers vast possibilities to the Third World. Solar batteries are here, and their potential scope is wide. Uranium-consuming reactors are but a passing phase, unless breeder plants are perfected, but, as Landsberg says, "Development of a successful commercial fusion process would knock out all long-term speculations on energy adequacy, and the odds on this happening within a generation or two are reasonably attractive." [57]

On this score few skeptics remain, and when it comes, one gallon of seawater could produce as much usable energy as 300 gallons of gasoline. The oceans are rich in deuterium, or heavy hydrogen, the primary fuel of the sun, which is bound to become the primary fuel of man. Reporting at the 1971 annual meeting of the National Academy of Sciences, University of California nuclear scientist Richard F. Post said that deuterium exists in sufficient quantity "to satisfy any conceivable energy demands for thousands of millions of years." [58] The price of obtaining it, he went on, "is so low that, as a fuel, deuterium would cost less than one percent of the present cost of coal, on a per-unit-of-energy basis."

If the deeper knowledge that the material needs of life support, even to the extent of 100 billion individuals, are unlimited appears as at least a partial contradiction of the contentions of Ridgeway and the Barclay group about privileged class fears for the world's resources, it only proves that privileges are blinding. Such a contradiction arises from the indisputable fact that populations are growing at a speed that will necessitate changes in the social order so unwelcome to those for whom the earth has already well provided. This does not preclude their desire for "progress."

Quite the contrary. Elites, excluding those who have become hopelessly crippled and disconsolate by apparitions of the "impenetrable mudslide," wish to help the poor, far more than the poor imagine that they can help themselves. But the single condition, for which no contradiction can ever be found, is the nonnegotiability of their claim to an eternal hold on the sources of all wealth, power, and prestige.

The president of the World Bank, Robert S. McNamara, who represents the most advanced segment of the neo-Malthusian view, sees these larger dimensions in more or less the same way, if not in the same language. McNamara, the Ford man, the Secretary of Defense, who is known more for the "ecological" damage he helped bring to Vietnam than for his role in stirring up the ecological hysteria in the United States,* does not himself suffer from the fever. In 1970, elaborating the bank's policy of using aid to underdeveloped countries as leverage for the extension of population control, he told his Board of Governors that the only thing threatened by the population explosion was a social order "morally acceptable" to those he believes competent to make such judgments. His actual words were as follows:

> The profound concern we must feel for the rapid growth of population stems precisely from the menace it brings to any morally acceptable standard of ex-

* Ridgeway writes: "At the heart of the ecology movement is the pollution-control industry. Its growth is tied to a series of policies initiated during Robert McNamara's tenure as Secretary of Defense. . . . McNamara's theory was that large corporations are best organized to solve the 'problems' of . . . the environment." Through a system of Pentagon training grants, Ridgeway continues, McNamara directly involved the aerospace companies in studying pollution problems. "As a result they now receive a quarter of the Federal government's research funds for water-pollution control."

> istence. We do not want fewer children born into the world because—to quote the more extreme critics of population policy—we do not like their color, or fear their future enmity, or suspect that they will in some unspecified way encroach upon the high consumption standards of already industrialized lands. . . . There are really no material obstacles to a sane, manageable, and progressive response to the world's development needs. The obstacles lie in the minds of men. . . . The conclusion is inevitable: we must apply at the world level that same moral responsibility, that same sharing of the wealth, that same standard of justice and compassion, without which our own national societies would surely fall apart.[59]

No change, just more of the same, best, American style.

Thus, the full range of the neo-Malthusian interpretation of past, present, and future may perhaps be perceived. Sometimes, in the outspokenness of more than a few professors and the whispers of their more silent partners, the racialist, reactionary origins of this view are clear. Sometimes in the formulations of more sophisticated men, it is in the vanguard of a certain kind of progress. Here it is against the green revolution; there it sides with it. Antidevelopment while being pro. Negating negations, belying its own assertions, the ally of everyone, opposed to the enemies of all. But the fundamental cry is: up with the status quo.

Under this morass the rumbling giant lies. The mood it has made, its prevalence and potency, should be borne in mind by those who are concerned with the problems of substance that keep him shackled in the earth.

IV

REAL PROBLEMS

DEMOGRAPHIC PRESSURE, inordinately accelerated, has created an inescapable need for a global green revolution to feed a future population that must inevitably grow to a number much higher than today's. This revolution, in its turn, has generated, or laid bare, an agglomeration of concrete problems new and old, of varying complexities, interrelationships, and dynamic intensities. To the measure that the revolution proceeds, these problems are surmountable. Insofar as it is hindered, run aground, or otherwise slowed, so much more inflammable do the problems become. Where the revolution has not yet started, there it is most certain to come.

Only war on a worldwide scale, genocide of unprecedented proportions, or whatever other means man may invent to bring on himself a qualitative rise in death rates (all distinct possibilities) can forestall this run of affairs—but even then for only the time it might take to return to the present condition. As for birth rates, to the extent that they can be made to decline, the unhappy status quo may be retained, but sooner or later (barring the total destruction of man) the higher numbers will be reached. This much the mysterious population explosion assures—at least for the next hundred years.

The tangible problems of the green revolution, like every human dilemma, ride a tortuous rail to the tiny, conservative kingdom where all social power ultimately resides and all realities emerge. No matter what the issue may be, it is hooked inextricably to another of a higher degree of variability until, in the end, it runs headlong into an impasse which is incapable by definition of being anything less. The simplest problem may be solved by one or another means, but whatever the means, when it is set into motion, it calls up problems of a more intricate order requiring means of greater sophistication. The process continues up the line until at last the impasse is reached. It is this impasse—the old kingdom of vested interests—that is now being cajoled, battered, and rammed, though concession is hardly in view.

Let us abstract the sequence of events. Given the present rate of population growth and the life-support capacities building up from the new technologies, problems of a primary nature arise in the sphere of ecology. They are more or less resolvable by scientific and technical, economic and social, and political means. The scientific and technical problems involved can often be dealt with by the last three. The economic and social sectors are highly interreactive, and while one may be employed to alleviate problems that lie in the other, or combined to reduce the stresses inhering in both, more frequently they can be ameliorated by political action. The political sphere encompasses all the problems of man; but what is politics if not the right hand of his institutions, the structure that contains and apportions by tradition, law, and armed force all the power at his command? Thus any problem leans on all of them, and all of them press on the guarded heavy doors of institutionalized power. The green revolution (driven relentlessly by the population explosion) presses and leans harder than ever before.

Consider ecology. The four main technologies of today's green revolution—induced mutation, mechanization, irrigation, and chemical control—raise a set of problems that disturb the ecosystem, directly and indirectly.

The fact that superwheat and miracle rice, to mention only the key features of the new technology, are the result of mutations, man-made or otherwise, brings on the risk that one journalist calls "the imminent danger of becoming stranded on a genetic razor's edge."[1] The march of the green revolution across the continents means the replacement of ancient, tried and true crop varieties—a conquest of necessity that conceivably could destroy the very genetic base that gave life to the new races of dwarfs. The new plants, being new, have not been tested by time. Although bred for resistance to known diseases, they are unlike traditional plants, which have gained their defenses through thousands of years of natural selection, and by their very survival have demonstrated their staying power, at least in their home environment. The dwarfs are a cosmopolitan breed, members of a kind of jet set. They have no home ground, moving as they do from one country to another, exposing themselves to all manner of plant disease. Moreover, while the old varieties were rich in diversity, the new tend to be of one cloth, a single blanket being thrown down around the world—or so the story sometimes goes.[2]

The argument of the critics of this publicized condition —particularly the population controllers and their ecological wing—suggests that were the new plants suddenly plagued by some unknown disease, for which they might have no defense, they could be wiped out to the last grain. The entire blanket could be consumed, causing global famine in the first act of an immense world catastrophe (William Paddock predicts: ". . . surely to be seen in the 1970s").[3] Further, the new plants drive out those that had previously occupied the land, and were they to fail, it is said, the old, trustworthy varieties would either have become extinct or would have to return to an irrevocably altered soil.

Memories of Ireland are thrown upon a screen. Ireland—that is, the Irish poor—by the 1840s had become dependent on a single species of potato introduced from the New World.[4] When in 1845 and 1846 it was struck by the blight, then an unknown disease, crop failure was widespread. Famine was followed by typhus, and a million Irishmen died.

In the exaggerated, mirror-writing neo-Malthusian interpretation of this disaster, the potato had permitted the Irish population to expand from 2 million to 8.5 million, only to be eventually halved by Malthus' checks of starvation, poverty, and disease. And all this, says Ehrlich for one, relating it to the green revolution, "presents a grim warning of what may lie in store for many developing nations."[5]

To learn that British-ruled Ireland was forced during the famine to export its unaffected grain and meat production (to uphold the principle of free trade); that reliance on potato-growing was literally the only possibility open to a people pushed to the last resort by the most vulgar exploitation; that this was compelled not by overpopulation but by the hated Corn Laws (in contradiction of the principle of free trade) and by a land-tenure system of subdividing holdings to "insanely fragmented" bits to increase rents and tithes; for this information one must consult the history books, as it is not usually remembered.

But no matter. The "lumper" potato is no ancestral prototype of the green revolution, and we have traveled a piece since the mid-1840s.

To be sure, the 50 million acres or so of green revolution land is vulnerable to some unknown pest or disease yet to evolve (as were the old plants displaced). But it is simply untrue that superwheat, miracle rice, and all the other high-yielding varieties are of one stripe, and that an attack here or there implies the death of even a significant fraction of all. The new seeds have been and continue to be bred in thousands of varieties, crossed with local, traditional breeds to incorporate their most desirable genes. At Punjab Agricultural University, to take one example, in the spring of 1971 some 5,000 to 7,000 different species of high-yielding plants were being cultivated experimentally.[6] If it is believed that the chances of Indians' doing anything right are "about zero," one may have cause for alarm. But in fact India has installed a highly effective national surveillance system, designed to give ample early warning of the approach of plant disease, and the protection technology for containment.[7] India's top green revolution scientist, Dr. Swaminathan, wonders why foreign pessimists who deprecate the new seeds think "we are unaware of the genetic dangers and the means to manage them. I guess some people just don't like to receive good news."[8]

As for the removal by the penetration of the new seeds of their genetic base—the hardy, highly differentiated, but less efficient plants handed down by natural selection—much can be done to preserve it. This rich tapestry of variability is far more than a museum piece; it could be a fail-safe system against unforeseeable calamity, even a nuclear war, and it represents a vital genetic resource for future plant breeders. Some species have already been irrevocably lost in past folly, though this has hardly jeopardized the usefulness of the remainder. In the 1920s the Russians began collecting plant types, and since then an increasing number of "gene banks" have been established, such as the one at Fort Collins in the Rocky Mountains.[9] The genetic stock of hundreds of thousands of plant species is already banked in cold storage. Yet, as might be expected, this is not nearly enough. Dangerously little research has been done on the viability of genetic material stored in this way, and the collections themselves are far from exhaustive.

The green revolution, however, rather than intensifying the peril, has stimulated worldwide action on this problem and many others associated with plant-breeding technology. Governments—notably the United States, East Germany, Japan, and the Soviet Union—as well as the FAO and the Rockefeller Foundation—are moving into this field. Funds, as is often the case, are insufficient, but induced mutation technology, which is highly responsive to capital investment in research and development, is clearly on a very low order among the fundamental issues of the green revolution.

This is less true of irrigation and chemical control, still less of mechanization.

As every Polycrates must have his Nemesis, irrigation technology labors under the myth of the Aswan Dam. For American ecologist LaMonte Cole, *this* is the "ultimate disaster," at least for Egypt.[10] For Ehrlich, any high school student could have predicted that the dam would ruin the Nile Delta, which, he says, it is now doing.[11] Yet the Egyptians, after several years of reflection, went ahead with building the dam, perhaps, Ehrlich might say, because not very many Egyptians ever go to high school.

In reply, one need only quote from a study made by the British publication *The Economist,* which itself had earlier helped to perpetuate the myth. "In planning the high dam," it says, "the drawbacks were carefully calculated—even if they were given little publicity. . . . All of the [ill-effects] were foreseen, and only the erosion of the banks of the Nile has turned out to be more serious than was expected." [12] The British study estimates the benefits brought by the dam as increasing Egypt's national income on the order of $500 million annually, through greater agricultural productivity, land reclamation, flood control, improved Nile navigation, and hydroelectric power. The average rice crop and exports have already risen by over 50 percent, and Egypt is now self-sufficient in corn. The advent of perennial irrigation means that up to three crops a year can now be harvested from an additional 1 million acres. Irrigation from the dam has allowed Egypt's total cultivated area to be expanded by 10 percent. The dam will further permit the fulfillment of all of Upper Egypt's irrigation needs, with water left over to irrigate a million additional acres reclaimed from southern desert land.

All this from *The Economist.* Further, it feels that the power from the high dam, which is to electrify 5,000 villages over the next five years, could be of "transcendent importance," good news to many of the dam's detractors. It says:

> The electrical revolution in the countryside . . . should help to alleviate the still desperate problem of the rising birth rate: not so much because it will enable the villagers to sit up at night reading or watching tele-

vision rather than procreating as because it will reduce the importance of manual labor—which still persuades the *fellahin* of the value of having large families.

Such are the potentials of irrigation,[13] the *sine qua non* of the green revolution. The demands of the new seeds on water technology, which cannot cease until desalinization and long-range delivery systems become an economic reality, *do,* however, disturb the environment, often seriously. They cause earthly and human ills. Diverting river water onto the land, for example, raises the subsoil water table, and as water nears the surface, it inhibits the growth of plant roots by waterlogging. Worse, through evaporation, a residue of salts is left in the soil, ultimately rendering it unfit for cultivation. This condition, however, is easily remediable.[14] The sinking of tube wells to tap the water table directly brings about the opposite effect. The level is lowered, and the fresh water washes down the salts below the soil. Such small-scale irrigation wells are a key strategy of the green revolution. They cost about $1,500 each, a negligible economic factor considering the manifold increase in productivity returned. Hundreds of thousands of tube wells were installed in the late 1960s on green revolution land, and it appears that a combination of large- and small-scale systems can redress whatever imbalance man's intervention in the hydrological cycle might incur.

A graver ecological effect of interfering with the natural movements of waterways is the spread of a highly debilitating, chronic human disease. At the Aswan Dam it is called *bilharzia;* the Chinese know it as "snail fever"; its medical name is schistosomiasis, and now, having overtaken receding malaria, it ranks as one of the world's most prevalent tropical ailments.

The disease, caused by a snail-borne parasite, which penetrates the skin and eventually damages internal organs, is said to afflict 250 million people,[15] mostly the rural poor of Asia and Africa. Its incidence has increased as a result of river irrigation. The organisms thrive in such systems both in the water and on the wet croplands, because of their close proximity to human populations. Unlike seasonal irrigation by flooding or rainfall, perennially irrigated land perpetuates the parasitic relationship, which when broken keeps the disease from spreading and the snail population down. Schistosomiasis, however, can be cured by drugs and prevented by hygienic methods. It is rarely fatal, although by weakening its victim, it certainly shortens his life; and were it not for the death-wish features of population control, its eventual demise—like malaria and many other tropical diseases—would be virtually assured.

It can scarcely be doubted that the environmental problems originating from the world's irrigation requirements will submit to the powers of technology, and that the advance of technology is here, too, dependent on capital inputs. The problems associated with capital resources and capital formation are another matter, however. The water needs of the green revolution appear to be rising much faster than funding capacities under the present inequitable system of capital flow and distribution. This is not the same as saying that the necessary wealth is nonexistent. It is simply being used for other purposes, such as maintaining nuclear arsenals, puppet states, and counterinsurgency wars.

The United Nations Economic Commission for Asia and the Far East (ECAFE) estimated in 1971 that Asia's water supplies would have to double by 1980 to keep abreast of its requirements.[16] It is not water that is the missing ingredient; it is the tens of billions of dollars needed for water-resource development. How those accustomed to the luxuries of overkill intend to finance universal irrigation, which means the desalting and dispatch of seawater—a technology already well developed, if not in politically economic terms—is something yet to be revealed. In the meantime, illusions of controlling populations prevail.

Chemical agricultural technology is likewise attacked as causing great damage. The green revolution makes heavy use of inorganic fertilizers, though only for the sake of convenience. It matters little whether the nutrients be "chemical" or "organic,"[17] in spite of widespread notions that organic nutrients are more "natural." Excrement, animal or human, sometimes called "night soil" and once known as "dressing," is not the favored dish of plants. The organic portion of this kind of nourishment is merely the shell, which plants peel and throw away. Plants require—apart from carbon, hydrogen, and oxygen—nitrogen, potassium, phosphorous, and much smaller servings of ten other elements. Dung and composts add nothing to the formula. Inorganic fertilizers are odorless, far more vigorous, long-lived, and come wrapped in a package. What is at issue is the quantity involved, the sources of supply, and the effects of fertilizer on the environment.

One estimate projects inorganic fertilizer use as tripling by the end of this century to satisfy human food needs.[18] To provide well for a future population of 100 billion, production—in the unlikely event of almost two centuries of technological stagnation—would have to increase perhaps 100 times the present world output of some 60 million metric tons a year. This might appear as a monumental drain on natural resources, but, in fact, the three main elements—nitrogen, potassium, and phosphorous—for which any fear of scarcity might be raised, are rather abundant.[19]

Nitrogen, which makes up 70 percent of the earth's air, is literally inexhaustible, since it is naturally recycled. Tapping the 75 million pounds of nitrogen that lie over every acre of the earth's surface, incidentally, required the development of a technology once thought to be impossible. It was this particular pessimism that accounted for Crookes's prediction of global starvation by 1930, as well as forecasts of doom by men less renowned, who were watching the singular nitrate deposits in Chile being mined to exhaustion. But the German scientist Fritz Haber turned the trick of fixing nitrogen from the air in 1914 with a process the political economy could easily afford.

Potassium, which is today extracted in the form of potash, and phosphorous, which is taken from phosphate ores, recycle naturally, too, but at a rate too slow to supply current needs. Potash reserves, however, are immense; Canada alone possesses known quantities sufficient for thousands of years. Identified phosphate deposits have been estimated as adequate for the next thousand years at present rates of consumption, or several hundred years at higher levels of exploitation. But potash and phosphate are not the only source of these elements. They are merely the most economical, because of their concentration. The amount of phosphorous in the sea, which grows as a result of erosion, is inestimable, as are most of the minerals needed by man that can be found in the oceans. The economics of mining the sea is another problem, however, another thorn in the side of the present social order.

Inorganic fertilizers are damned by an unlearned consensus, which forgets or does not know that the "organic" variety, if it were used to achieve the same benefits as results from the employment of the former, would pollute to precisely an equal degree. It is quite fanciful, however, to suggest that the spreading of animal droppings, the treated sewage of cities, and like materials could come anywhere near satisfying the world's plant nutrient needs. In any event, the positive effects of intensive fertilizer use on the environment far outweigh the negative.[20] For example, it is untrue, notwithstanding the thunder of the environmentalists, that the friendly earthworm is dying out as fertilizers spread. Although it is a simple matter to demonstrate the lethal effects of some compounds in inorganic fertilizer when brought into contact with an individual worm, only a very small portion of the worm population ever comes near the offending substance. Instead, its total environment is enriched by the increased supply of organic material afforded through fertilization, and it is an established agronomic principle that the size and numbers of earthworms invariably grow as soils are brought from a low to high level of fertility through fertilization.

Intensive fertilization also makes the following contributions to the environment: Soils are rendered more friable, tillable, and receptive to water; farming efficiency and crop quality are greatly improved; soil erosion is retarded and hence silting and other forms of water pollution are abated; the use and conservation of water are more effective; the purification of the atmosphere is enhanced through increased plant growth, which absorb larger amounts of carbon dioxide and other pollutants such as sulfur dioxide, and release of greater quantities of oxygen.[21]

Moreover the long-term effects of inorganic fertilizer use are already known. The experimental Broadbalk fields of Rothamsted, which have been fertilized chemically since 1843, are more productive now than at any time in the recorded past, and Denmark's Askov agricultural station has demonstrated inorganic fertilizer to be superior to equivalent applications of organic over a fifty-year period.

The greatest danger from intensive fertilizer use comes from improper handling, and there is evidence that excessive application may cause deterioration of the quality of water, with possible hazards to human health and certain other aspects of the environment. It should be emphasized, however, that the use of fertilizers in quantities greater than required is a "luxury" only the United States and other nations of wealth can afford. In the countries of the green revolution the opposite is true: fertilizers are very much underemployed and the rates at which they will increase will not nearly approach those that have troubled the United States.

Nevertheless, the residues of these chemicals are eventually washed into bodies of water, and they contain some of the substances that can be shown to pollute drinking water, kill fish, and cause the enfeeblement of ponds, lakes, rivers, and streams by the process of eutrophication.

In the latter event, algae, fertilized by accumulating nitrates and phosphates, multiply swiftly, consume the water's oxygen, and kill off the fish. This is the cycle that wrote the celebrated ecological saga of Lake Erie, but eutrophication is not—though some environmentalists seem to believe otherwise—a recent phenomenon. It has been occurring since the beginning of time, which is how vast peat bogs were formed countless ages ago. The metabolism of lakes is influenced less by man's activities than by their depth, shape, temperatures, and geographic location, and it is therefore possible to see lakes surrounded by farms, some in the advanced stages of eutrophication, others with none at all.

How much eutrophication and other forms of water pollution can be attributed to agricultural technology and how much to the chemical discharge into the waters of industrial wastes and detergents (and how much through natural imbalances in ecosystems) is a question sterilely debated by narrow, private interests on all sides. It is of greater significance that control of at least the agricultural excesses involved is attainable at the present time and the possibility of a residue-free fertilizer technology is hardly far-fetched.[22]

Omar Khayyám said that the rose "never grows so red . . . as where some buried Caesar bled." That was because blood, the Biblical fertilizer, contains some of the same plant nutrients as inorganic fertilizer, which makes the green revolution so lush. This nourishment, however, does not as yet discriminate against weeds, which flourish on green revolution land. Moreover, lush plant growth can support a larger population of insects and other pests, and, were it not for chemical pesticides and weedicides, Crookes's prediction, if overdue, would assuredly one day come true.

The case against pesticides of the DDT group, the organochlorine compounds, grows less and less convincing, as has been suggested in the previous chapter. For some time, respectable scientists everywhere have been backing away from apocalyptic utterances about DDT. The exhaustive work of the FAO-WHO Codex Alimentarius Commission fully agrees with the view of the United States Surgeon General and others, including those already cited, that the traces of the chemical found in human tissue, as well as in mothers' milk, have no etiological relationship with any known human disease, including cancer and genetic changes.[23]

A recent report by the FAO provides documentation that ought to dispel some of the more popular notions about DDT. For one thing, if the entire population of Antarctic Adelie penguins contained as much DDT as those studied and found to bear small measures of the substance, the total burden of DDT in the 10 million animals would be only about 8.5 ounces.[24] For another, one need not postulate a thin-eggshell-due-to-DDT thesis to explain the decline of the bald eagle and a few other large birds of prey in the United States. Ornithologists have been reporting a reduction of the populations of these animals since the 1890s, long before DDT was introduced, and official records kept at the Hawk Mountain Sanctuary in Pennsylvania since 1934—still prior to the introduction of DDT—confirm this observed trend.[25]

Norman Borlaug staunchly opposes the critics of DDT. He argues boldly that the substance remains indispensable for our health and happiness and, turning back a phrase often served up by the neo-Malthusians, that a total ban on its use would result in "starvation and political chaos" throughout much of the globe.[26] The powerful lobby trying to ban it, he says, is going on "bits of unsubstantiated data and questionable ethics."[27] Led by the Sierra Club, the National Audubon Society, and the Environmental Defense Fund—the latter's motto being "Sue the bastards"—this lobby, according to Borlaug, is made up mostly of "bird watchers thrilling to the song of the meadowlark, urbanites rediscovering the beauties of nature, and other confused people obeying some basic animal instinct to join hysterical movements."[28]

True or not, it is of fundamental interest that Borlaug's brief is strong in scientific terms. He and others attribute much of the present confusion to highly sophisticated methods of chemical analysis of recent innovation. Where the level of detection used to be one part per million before gas chromatography was developed in 1956, it is now on the order of one part per billion, or even a few parts per trillion, which of course would have gone unnoticed twenty years ago. But, as one senior scientist recently asked, "How reliable is the test?" To illustrate the point that such sensitive technology is far from foolproof, soil samples sealed since 1910 were tested for chemical pesticides in the DDT family.[27] Traces were found in 32 of 34 samples—yet no chemical pesticides were in use in 1910, nor were they developed until nearly thirty years later.[29] Gas chromatography technology, says American biochemist Thomas Jukes, can easily mistake many other nonpesticide compounds for DDT, rendering such tests highly dubious.[30] Further, there is a danger of contamination from other sources, which is why the *New Scientist* calls collecting and analyzing traces of organochlorines a "tricky business." [31]

To be sure, no one advocates that mankind wallow in DDT, or that it is our best hope for survival. That DDT is a killer and has killed animals other than target species cannot be ignored. Like fertilizers, its residues run into the waters, and worse, they travel by air, permeating every part of the atmosphere. Birth defects that appeared in Vietnamese children following the United States's herbicidal "defoliation" campaign in their country are also highly suggestive, since such malformations have been similarly induced experimentally in rats.[32]

Most experts, including United Nations bodies established to study pesticide use, support the *proper* handling of DDT. They forthrightly oppose an outright ban, while favoring research for an integrated approach to pest control in agriculture. Integrated control, which is gaining more and more supporters, including Borlaug, implies the use of a package technology of chemical and other means ranging from viral and bacteriological insect killers, insect-destructive parasites to nuclear methods and perhaps best of all, breeding pest-resistant plants. Integrated control is as yet uneconomic in terms of the given economy, but it is here that much promising, if barely noticed, progress has been made in recent years; and it is here—not in faddism, rhetoric, or propaganda—that solutions appear to lie. Until they can be found and applied, the introduction of pesticides into the environment cannot but increase at a rate at least as high as that of the population explosion.

There will be many DDT-harboring fish, sick waterways, flawed irrigation systems, and foolhardy losses of the genetic material of plants. But on a worldwide scale these ecological problems, as well as those brought on by the tractor and farm machinery in general—that is, contributions to air pollution by the combustion of fossil fuels and, more important, to soil erosion by enhancing the power to extend land cultivation—can be adjusted by technical means. In absolute terms, as an immediate threat to the whole environment, they are of a rather minor nature. The earth could absorb all the poisons spewed forth in the past with the impunity of a man suffering the bite of a single mosquito. The real peril lies not in any shortcomings of the corrective powers of technology, or any dearth in the man-made wealth by which it is fueled, but in a structural inability to settle the indirect issues that rise like the phoenix through the social medium to the highest affairs of men. It is this impotence that permits the repetition of known folly to pass unconfronted in ever larger numbers.

In no way, it seems, can this be illustrated better for our purposes than by following the ramifications of the secondary problems that emerge from the mechanization technology of the green revolution. The other instruments of the revolution reviewed above are also driven by inevitable circumstance on a spiral to higher complexities, but in a more abstract manner. Further, mechanization, or labor-releasing automation, is far from being the sole cause of the pressure brought to bear on the top. One must carefully follow the swath of history, at least since the beginnings of the industrial revolution—when the poor countries of today were no less underdeveloped than those they were coerced by brute force to enrich—to observe the roots of the present poverty of nations. But almost equally edifying is the simple progression rapidly transforming mankind from an overwhelmingly rural to an overwhelmingly urban creature, a loaded social phenomenon, which pivots on the growth of agricultural automation.[33]

At the beginning of the eighteenth century, some 10 percent of the world's population were living in cities, with 90 percent ensconced in what Marx once called "the idiocy of rural life." Sometime early in the twenty-first century the figures will have been reversed if the trend continues. In the absence of social change, the human race will have become predominantly a species of slum dwellers —Frantz Fanon's "spearhead" of political revolution and a *Lumpenproletariat* to others. The world's urban poor, numbering in the several billions, will have been concentrated inside the very precincts of power, having entered in the Trojan horse of the 300-year rural exodus. What kind of "spearhead" they may prove to be is hardly foreseeable, Fanon notwithstanding, and leaving "the idiocy" behind them does not imply a march toward enlightenment and wisdom, although Marx assumed it would. It does, however, indicate the dimensions to which the challenge of the green revolution might grow.

The formula, which has been operating for so long, is fairly uncomplicated. Demographic insistence leads to higher efficiencies in the man-to-land ratio. Higher efficiency better exploits one man's labor, rendering the numbers needed before redundant. Redundancy gives way to unemployment, and the unemployed peasants are lured by the call of the cities, where opportunity is said to abound.

This was the process that created the black ghettos of America, leaving a once-rural nation with a farm population now a mere 3.5 percent of the total. It was also the process that provided the urbanized, proletarianized labor force in the quantity and density that helped make the United States the leading industrial power in the world.

Unlike the American experience, however, as well as the European and Japanese, the Third World countries have now been caught in the same tidal movement without an industrial base capable of absorbing the surplus labor of the rural exodus. Industrialization and economic takeoff in the West *preceded* the arrival of the job-hunters from the countryside, and many times they were welcomed in the city, if more for the cheap price of their labor than from brotherly love. In the poor countries the immigrants are arriving much *in advance* of industrialization, and are rarely welcomed at all.

When farm mechanization, a relatively new phenomenon, is added to the equation, this distortion of the situation, as it differs between the rich countries and the poor, becomes truly grotesque. Whereas mechanization in the West was a *result* of the rural exodus, the same population shift in the Third World is taking place with mechanization as a *cause*. Agricultural machine technology, a product of the industrialization dynamic, was introduced in the rich countries primarily to compensate for the depletion of human labor from the countryside—the flight of the people who had gone to the cities to make the very machines involved. In the underdeveloped countries, where the rural population is growing in spite of the exodus, the technology is merely added to the efficiency-redundancy side of the formula, which has a powerful effect in enlarging the end result. Thus in Latin America, where the effects of runaway mechanization are worst, the urban population is growing three times faster than the rural, at a rate that will make some big cities double their inhabitants in slightly more than ten years.

Of such are made the squalid, seething *barriadas* of the Spanish-speaking poor, the *favelas* of Brazil, the *bidonvilles* of French Africa, and the *jhuggi* shantytowns of Calcutta and Bombay. These Third World dregopolises are expanding not as much from "natural" growth as from the blind-alley flow to the city from the farm. In many big cities of the poor countries, invading squatters, voting with their backsides against the sanctity of private property and the civil order on which it stands, already outnumber those in the city proper. By the end of the century, to live in a Third World slum will be not the exception but the rule.

That this is a man-made feature of the population explosion already exploding is not difficult to discern. Anyone who has ever endured the interminable bus ride from Santa Cruz Airport in Bombay to, say, the Ritz Hotel in the center of town, has seen the red flags flying from the million-population shantytowns, which begin but a few hundred yards from the runways. In 1971 the slogan slapped down on the walls was, "Socialism means freedom and progress." What kind of socialism, what kind of progress, is less readily perceived. The crucible of slum life, where all manner of tradition and values, good and bad, are trampled in the dust, does not make much for human kindness or an understanding of the plight of historic man. It is a cause of unrest, hatred, and violence, and more often than not it brings on an escalation of oppression and the letting of human blood.

Misery is not the missing element of social revolution and the establishment of justice; and the Fanonites and Marxists have a poor record indeed in their foretelling of a special mission for the poor, proletarianized, or otherwise. Yet, as one writer has observed, "Concentration in urban centers gives revolutionary cadres a position closer to the management of the society and the conduct of its political life." [34] Against this urban explosion, free condoms, loop fittings, and the barkers of vasectomy sideshows are of no avail.

The reason that no amount of birth control can influence the mushrooming unemployment problem in the underdeveloped countries, which in some cases is already up to 30, 40, and even 50 percent of the labor force and which is growing even faster than the world's population, is quite elementary. The hundreds of millions of young people who between now and the late 1980s will be entering the poor countries' job market, only to be turned away, are beyond the pill. They are already born, every last one of them, and they may be expected to lean very hard on the political economy.

The green revolution, on the other hand, can do much to alleviate this problem and brake the rural exodus. As was noted in Chapter II, the transition to higher levels of agriculture invariably requires more labor. The use of irrigation, chemical controls, and primarily multiple cropping, which demand that the land be worked the year around, can provide continuous employment for rural manpower.[35] In "overpopulated" India the sudden shift to green revolution farming precipitated severe labor shortages in some parts of the country, with farm wages rising above those in the city. Moreover thousands of peasants in the tropics, by switching to the new seeds, have been pulled abruptly from the mire of subsistence farming, finding themselves with a marketable surplus production. An expansion of marketing requires road-building, storage, and transportation facilities, all labor-intensive activities. Still more, a general increase in agricultural productivity generates the capital for rural electrification programs and the incentive for agriculturally based industries to relocate in the countryside, bringing with them money and jobs.

All this is, in fact, actually happening in countries where the green revolution is spreading, and the labor market is expanding accordingly. At a certain point, however, an increase in wealth among green revolution landowners brings about the logical imperative to introduce heavy farm machinery—tractors, harvesters, threshers, etc.—and derive the considerable personal gains these devices afford. A single combine, which in some of these countries must be purchased on the black market, can do the harvesting and threshing work of a hundred men.

To combat this, development economists, United Nations organizations, and others have begun to advocate a policy of "selective" mechanization, the theory evidently being that there are good and bad machines. This is tantamount to asking people to give up sex during Lent; some will and some will not. There is nothing "bad" about a combine; it is a remarkable machine, a great liberator of human toil. What is needed is not a restructuring of attitudes toward imagined traits possessed by one or another machine, but a restructuring of the land-tenure systems in the underdeveloped world. A single combine may throw a hundred men and women out of work, but the mismanaged or unexploited holdings of a South American *latifundista* could, when rationalized, not simply socialized, provide jobs for thousands.

At the question of land ownership one comes at last to

the final social impasse. It is the halfway house that separates all the nitty-gritty technoeconomical problems from the interlock of sacred custom, inviolable tradition, and sumptuary laws that precludes their solution. In the underdeveloped countries, in spite of endless, tiresome variations of styles of tenure, those who control the land control the people, their bodies, their minds, and their souls.

Land-reform specialist Solon Barraclough, of Cornell University, writes: [36] "In poor agrarian societies, land is the main source of wealth. As a result, the control over land largely determines income, wealth, and power in backward agricultural areas. Income from land, however, cannot be realized without labor." Labor is supplied by the peasant, and since the landowner is in this manner dependent on peasant labor, he must, if he wishes to continue in his position of privilege, redirect the wealth, power, and status he has arrogated to himself, and on which his society is founded, to assure that the required labor remains in his control. "Therefore," says Barraclough, "the distribution of property rights in land is necessarily accompanied by a system of interpersonal and intergroup relationships. *In brief, land ownership is closely associated with the power to make others do one's will.*" [37] Barraclough continues:

> These local social systems determine the power structure within which peasants must live and operate. They establish the penalties, incentives, and rewards peasants receive for changing their farming methods. They govern the distribution of income and wealth that may be generated by new agricultural technologies. They set the limits on the peasants' and farm laborers' participation in the development process.

To this, one may add the proposition, which has rarely been breached, that he who possesses such powers never relinquishes his claim that they belong only to him, not to those he commands. There is no reasoning, no appeal, no quantity of capital investment, foreign aid, and technical assistance capable of persuading him otherwise. Indeed, by a sociological phenomenon known as vertical allegiances,[38] by caste systems, alliances not among equals but cutting through social classes to ever-higher ranking personages—Mafia style—all the energy and riches a nation might have or acquire are used to fortify this established order. Every man or matter that may defy it is either coopted or diverted, transformed or emasculated, shelved or imprisoned, unheeded or destroyed. Governments of developed countries—non-Communist and Communist alike—foreign investors, and international organizations often deplore this state of affairs. And so do the very elitists involved. But in recording their deeds, not their words, its worldwide support is revealed. In this way is the status quo maintained.

Here is why the green revolution has often made the haves have more and the have-nots stand still. Here, too, are the origins of the long-standing fallacies about peasant passivity and "unwillingness" to change.* Nevertheless, the powers of the green revolution have, in some instances, proved greater than those of the "system," showing the opposite to be true. Studies in India make clear that impoverished peasants, given half a chance, have taken a

* Revolutionaries, from the Ché Guevarists and onward, as well as liberals and reactionaries, have all bought this myth. Francisco Juliao, who led the peasant leagues in northeast Brazil, has characterized the typical peasant as one who does "not act like a human being, but like a vegetable." This compares with the conservative view of American scholar Everett Rogers, who finds the peasants of Colombia "mentally degenerate." Marion Brown, of the University of Iowa, who has studied the subject, rejects this conception. He writes that the peasant is "as ready as other people to seize opportunities for both individual advancement and mutually advantageous collective action." His backwardness, says Brown, arises from the social conditions as outlined above.[39]

radical turn to the new technology. In the frustrations of securing even half a chance, however, they have also frequently been led to violence.

The oligarchies, the elites, and their clients, who represent an infinitesimally small percentage of the people in the underdeveloped world, have managed so far to quell disorder and retard social change. They continue to control the social sources of what men think and how they perform. Their activities unfold not on the land they so guardedly hold but at the power stations of their nation's universities, industries, embassies, ministries, and many times in the halls of the United Nations. They, and their generally less landed but far more influential counterparts in the advanced countries, who frequent similar places, are the incarnation of the social impasse. On their desks the real problems of the poor, economic and social development, and the green revolution converge, and go no further. And the problems pile up higher with each passing day.

Why this condition stands in men's way has been a subject of the first half of this book. How it proceeds in cold practice, and what may be done to ease it, if not to put it aside, is a subject of the second.

V

THE CASE OF INDIA

MAX WEBER, who linked the spectacular achievements of capitalism to the uniqueness of Protestant beliefs, placed Indian society outside the pale of the "rational organization" of men necessary to harness science and technology to economic and social development.[1]

The Indians, while they had invented the decimal system, had no "modern arithmetic or bookkeeping," he observed, and "a rational, systematic, and specialized pursuit of science, with trained and specialized personnel, has only existed in the West in a sense at all approaching its present dominant place in our culture."

The "stroke of genius" that had combined caste legitimacy with the *karma* doctrine of retribution through reincarnation—or what Weber called the "wheel of rebirths"—predisposed the Indians to endure or escape their world, never to change it. With an iron logic unto itself, this was a closed social system in which wealth, power, and prestige were indivisible. They were entirely invested in fatherlike figures who ruled not by representation but by charisma and the Hindu beliefs. Thus the Indian was "accursed to remain in a structure which made sense only in this intellectual context: its consequences burdened his conduct."

The inescapable conclusion was that India, for better or worse, was forever barred from the troubled Eden of "rational bourgeois capitalism."

Weber made his greatest contributions to sociological thought in the first decade of this century. By 1972, however, India was dismantling the old structure, tying itself to the highest forms of capitalist development, and riding science and technology out of the bind. Going forward on the green revolution, India in the past five years has been gnawing at the monolith of wealth, power, and prestige. To that extent it is becoming an open society, proving, for one thing, that population growth as the motive force for change can benefit development and, for another, that the wheel of rebirths is less mighty than the wheel of the machine.

Yet, while the new technology has perhaps done more to deny the legitimacy of the caste system than its legal abolition by Gandhi, the revolution is today being slowed. It is hindered not so much by oriental custom as by the world political economy. In a few muscular strides, India, so long synonymous with hunger and famine, has transcended its popular images. It has approached the global social impasse. Dynamic, potentially bountiful, filled with unassembled energies and marvels, and so eminently capable of greatness in Western terms, India is today the underdeveloped world's prime paradigm of the present limitations of the green revolution.

India is green revolution country *par excellence*. It has more land sown to superwheat and miracle rice,[2] for example, than the combined total of all the other non-Communist countries that have adopted the tropical technology.[2]

This as yet amounts to only 20 percent of its 135 million acres of farmland under wheat and rice, but the effect, compressed within a five-year period, has been felt hard in every corner of the country, and the momentum, in spite of braking, is bound to carry the new seeds far. In any case, the nation has undergone significant changes from which it is most difficult to retreat.

The ubiquitous critics, on the fair but here inappropriate Aristotelian theory that one swallow does not make a summer, raise doubts that this 20 percent figure may be interpreted as a revolution. But there is no need of conjecture about the impact the green revolution has had on India. It is measurable, and has been measured from every conceivable angle, in terms of hard figures, sentiment, and even blood.

The Indian green revolution, like most revolutions, came on a train of fortuitous circumstance; at another time it could not have had the outcome it had. The droughts of the mid-1960s, the worst in forty years, threw the leaders of state into panic. Crops were ruined, drinking water grew perilously scarce, and tens of millions of Indians had to queue at government stores for a handout of American grain. Men stood on the docks of Bombay and Calcutta straining their eyes for a convoy of 600 ships shuttling surplus wheat from the United States and depleting a stockpile the Americans said they had no intention to replenish.

Hitherto India had depended on U.S. surplus grains to fill in local shortfalls, giving a low priority to its own languishing agriculture. "Why should we bother?" an Indian official is reported to have remarked. "Our reserves are the wheat fields of Kansas." [3]

But this time had passed, and when the plain-spoken Paddock brothers predicted that the "black horse of famine would be riding through India" [4] before too long, the nation's leaders, we have it from a reliable source, were convinced. "Many of us," a member of parliament has said, referring to the Paddock forecasts, "thought that our country was losing its capacity to feed itself." [5]

Ironically it was the Paddocks and the more sensible but no less pessimistic Gunnar Myrdal and his widely read *Asian Drama,* who helped set the mood of desperation, which allowed the exotic green revolution to come to pass.[6] For on the other side of the coin, India over the years had been building up a highly competent agricultural science based on the American land-grant university system. This had gone all but unnoticed, but when Dr. Swaminathan presented the government with the chance that Borlaug's Mexican-based tropical technology might work in India, the power structure opened every door to let the green revolution through, hoping that it might save the day. This breakthrough in the normally rather inert Indian bureaucracy was perhaps the biggest "revolution" of all.

"Only science seemed to have all the answers to the problem of making India a viable state," Swaminathan said later, "and so, with the government ripe for change, we were able to move quickly and boldly." [7]

The hard-pressed farmers, too, proved willing to try anything promising, and when the startling results of the first trials were made known, a race for the new seeds was on.

"Farmers were paying for the new varieties literally by the kernel," says Ashok Thapar, an astute observer of the Indian agricultural scene. "Experimental plots . . . had to be guarded by armed sentries day and night because farmers were willing to go to any lengths just to obtain a handful of the new seed." [8]

Seed supply was to become less problematical some seasons later, but one can still see patches of green revolution land stripped of its plants by night-raiding peasants eager to give the dwarfs a try.

The spread of the green revolution in India, the rapid changeover from archaic to modern technologies, and the dramatic gains in productivity dispersed the clouds that had hung so heavily over the nation. They were replaced by a manic climate, in which for a few swift moments anything seemed within reach, at least among the nation's leaders.

The World Bank's India-watcher, Wolf Ladejinsky, made two trips through the northern state of Punjab early in 1969 and reported that the presence of the green revolution "was very much in evidence." He warned of impending social repercussions, some of which proved to be important, but in general he confirmed the wonder of it all. He wrote in the Indian review *Economic and Political Weekly:*

> Owner-farmers with irrigated land are making money hand over fist, and the bigger the farm the more they make; of the "burden" of taxation there is none to speak of; land values are spiralling; land rents are going up [illegally] . . . the demand for casual labor has increased and so have wages, and the landless laborer is somewhat better off than in the past . . .
>
> Regardless of whether an observer probes deeply or ever so lightly into the Punjab scene, the signal impression he is bound to carry away is one of the air of prosperity that permeates the State. Those bent on measuring everything quantitatively can feast on the 80–90 percent coverage of wheat land with high-yielding varieties, the doubling of yields per unit of land, the five to sixfold increase in fertilizer consump-

> tion between 1962–63, the 110,000 tube-wells, the steady increase in the number of tractors, the waiting lists of would-be tractor purchasers which stretches from here to there, the 5,000 threshers reportedly sold this past year, and so on, and so on. This and much else not statistically measurable . . . testify to Punjab's rural muscle. In fact, the mere sight of a profusion of tractors rumbling up and down a road creates the impression that Punjab "has done it." [9]

On my own visit exactly two years later to Punjab and neighboring states, although I was not as prepared as Ladejinsky, I, too, observed what he had seen, and it had become all the more magnified. Most of the figures he had used had been replaced by higher ones, and the waiting lists, while names were being deleted with the help of the black market, were longer than before. The roads were jammed tighter with tractors, although most were used more for transportation than for their intended purpose, and many, I learned, had been bought for no use at all other than to keep up with the Punjabi Joneses.

Some of the farmers who had made money "hand over fist" were now building new homes and swimming pools on their once less prosperous lands. Agricultural industries servicing and manufacturing farm inputs had moved into the state, making jobs for the landless. Indeed, there was a labor shortage in Punjab now. The state agricultural university was undergoing major expansion, construction in general was booming, and the Punjabis had gained a reputation of being not only hard-working but hard-drinking as well. They boasted of being ready to supply all the nation's wheat needs, and 60,000 Punjabis were being trained to take rice as a second crop and move in on the traditional market of the south.[10]

Complaints had a familiar ring often heard in the West—those of surplus production, inflation, inadequate price supports, and what to do with "black money" gained from evading taxes. Farming had become a tax haven, but by now most of the lands in the state had been saturated with the new seeds, which was one of the reasons the thrust of the green revolution in Punjab was running down.

In 1969, however, Ladejinsky had found quite another "fly in the ointment." [11] The real sharing in Punjab's agricultural revolution "is restricted to relatively few, perhaps only ten and surely not more than twenty percent of the farm households." Thus, he concluded, while the green revolution had done a "yeoman job" it was also an indirect cause of "the widening gap between the rich and the poor."

This was an observation—later developed by Ladejinsky and many other writers both foreign and domestic, including the government—that was foreseen as leading to a sharp increase in social tensions. Ladejinsky himself later refined his personal views, affirming that "peasant rebellion and chaos is unlikely, for the kind of poverty that wouldn't be tolerated in many another country is still tolerated in India." * [12] But this reassured few people in India, and in an unpublished document [13] drawn up by the Ministry of Home Affairs, the "widening gap" idea was highly elaborated. The green revolution, it was said, increased the relative disparity between rich and poor, which led to a sense of deprivation on the part of the poor. This quickly

* By 1971 Ladejinsky, or the World Bank, as the case may be, had apparently lost interest in the subject, claiming that a breakthrough in India had to come from "the other way around"—meaning population control. In this connection, he disclosed in an interview in New Delhi, the World Bank was currently engaged in drafting a multimillion-dollar scheme for population control in India—the first such World Bank project of its kind. Money was not an issue for this cause, he said; the question was how it could be best utilized.

became the prevailing explanation of the cause of agrarian unrest, which at that time had begun to erupt in violence.

Less than two months before Ladejinsky's first tour of India's north, forty-two persons had been burned to death in the south in a clash between landless peasant laborers and green revolution farmers who had refused to meet their wage demands. The farmers had been reaping the profits of the maiden harvest of miracle rice.[14] Forty-three "incidents" of this sort had been recorded that year (1968),[15] and in 1969, there were several hundred cases of the forcible occupation of land in West Bengal alone, totaling up to 300,000 acres, with many crop seizures and many killings and injuries.[16]

In November of that year, the prime minister went before the chief ministers of all the states, declaring that "the warning of the times is that unless the green revolution is accompanied by a revolution based on social justice the green revolution may not remain green."[17]

A national land-grab movement began to grow up around the avowedly violent Naxalites, a Maoist splinter group, which proceeded to organize guerrilla bands throughout the countryside. The Naxalites were said to be articulating the iniquities of the green revolution. In August, 1970, other leftist parties joined the movement; 100,000 so-called volunteers grabbed 30,000 acres.[18] There were 16,000 arrests.

In the meantime, however, the concept of the widening gap was shown to be too simplistic, more useful as an instrument of political "gapsmanship" than as an explanation of social realities. It was certainly true, as has almost always been the case, that the rich were getting richer and the poor relatively poorer, and that the process had been made more visible by the green revolution, but it rarely follows that this engenders political action. On the contrary, the trickle-down nature of capitalism, based on the perfectly valid idea that the greater the portions at the rich man's table, the larger the crumbs that fall from it, enhances rather than endangers social stability. Theories about relative justice, however correct, are less readily perceived than a 50 percent raise in a working man's pay—an increase the green revolution had often afforded. While Ladejinsky had accurately recorded that the "gap" in Punjab was greater than in any other part of rural India, that state had the least amount of agrarian unrest.

In fact, the more profound analyses of the economic and social effects of India's green revolution agreed that "the widening gap" had been all but obscured by the crumbs. In the first place, many economists and other specialists, such as I. J. Singh and Chadbourne Gilpatric,[19] of the Rockefeller Foundation in India, and a team of Indian researchers, showed that the green revolution had a high rate of adoption among small farmers—those with holdings of 7.5 acres or less. The new technology did not necessarily require economies of scale, and, as was the case, small farms could benefit from it, too, though not proportionately. The gap between them was still widening, but at a slower speed than before, and as for landless laborers, the green revolution was found to increase demand for their services by about 30 percent. Even mechanization could only cut this back by some 10 percent, and a study by AID in New Delhi revealed that because most Indian farms were small, the total automation of all holdings large enough to enjoy the economic advantages of heavy farm machinery would alter the situation only negligibly.[20]

In the second place, as research by Indian sociologists [21] helped clarify, the green revolution possessed the remarkable faculty of being able to absorb *and* exacerbate social tensions. It eased social unrest by distributing income a little less unfairly. In this narrow sense the green revolution was politically counterrevolutionary in that it permitted the established order to perpetuate itself by reducing the grievances of the poor. That social tensions were rising nonetheless was due, partially, to the green revolution's confinement to only some favored parts of the country, and to structural changes that had taken place in Indian society, caused to a certain extent by the same new technology. Thus the green revolution was operating on both sides of the political fence. Insofar as it helped to prop up the old order, stability was assured. To the measure that its benefits could not be extended—a function of its ability to *fortify* the establishment—order and stability were threatened—a function of its ability to *undermine* the establishment.

This circle of causation is raised to a higher level of complexity by a number of other factors. Though the green revolution may treat the economic ills of the poorer peasants, it excites their social aspirations, and, in Weberian terms, tends to "rationalize" their general outlook on life. The discovery that their plight was anything but foreordained by the Hindu gods has eroded beliefs in *karma* and the entire caste system. Casteism had been slowly worn down since India's independence by a wide range of modernizations, from universal suffrage to a pervasive outpouring of socialist rhetoric (India insists that it is building socialism). But the economic takeoff and the psychological recovery stimulated or abetted by the green revolution filled out all the tall talk and ideals with something that could be touched.

One of the more significant tangibles was cash, which for the first time came into the hands of millions of Indians accustomed to being rewarded for their toil in kind. Until the green revolution created labor shortages requiring the importation of farm workers from as far as a thousand miles away, the sleepy order of *jajmani* had been supreme. Every rural sector, in spite of legal bans, had been divided into several castes from the large landowner down to the village smith. Loyalties were tied from the very bottom to the very top. Youths were dependent on their elders; women, on men; and men, on the caste system. The landowner leased his fields to tenants and sharecroppers; the fields were worked by the landless and serviced by "untouchable" handymen—all in exchange for food. Such was the substance of placid, unchanging village life; no two carpenters, no two blacksmiths, had common bonds; each owed his well-being, such as it was, to the man above.

But the high profitability of the green revolution proved more honorable than ancient custom. The landlords, seeking to reap the gains of the new technology for themselves, drove out their tenants and their sharecroppers, rendering them common farmhands. Industry, to take advantage of untaxed agriculture, bought out small holders. And when local peasant labor became insufficient, out-of-staters had to be temporarily employed, and the old debts of loyalty could only be discharged in cash.

Surveying this development in an article called "Green for Danger," the *Far Eastern Economic Review* wrote in October, 1970:

> The Green Revolution is destroying the social significance of land and labor, "freeing" it to be mobilized by market forces and invested in profitable enterprises.
>
> As this process proceeds, the peasantry will be cut off from its cultural anchorage and the vertical ties that once held the landlord and tenant in a symbiotic relationship will be severed. The landlord who once

> protected his tenants by providing credit and aid will follow the dictates of an impersonal market and maximize his returns regardless of the immediate social consequences. This is already occurring in India . . .[22]

Traditional society was being destroyed, said the review, and replaced by a belief "that all factors of production, land, labor, and capital are for sale, not use." This trend was carried still further when political parties on the make discovered that the "free" migrant laborers, unfettered by local traditions, could readily be organized and opposed against the long entrenched. Such was the case in Punjab, for example, where the normally conservative Congress Party politicized farm labor against the Akali Dal movement, which itself had become established by championing the interests of the large farmers against the dominant local leaders.[23]

Cash, which became accessible not only to the landless but also to small owners moving on the new technology from subsistence farming into the market, changed consumption patterns, made the people more mobile and more attuned to new times. More important, agriculture moved from a stagnant social situation to a dynamic one, a spiraling interplay of new demands and higher social consciousness.

Of this and the indispensable support of political elites, social disquietude is made. Oddly enough, it was not "the system," contrary to what has often been asserted, that was the cause of rural unrest; rather, the breaking up of casteism, that long-standing "stroke of genius," has hastened India's link-up with the world political economy in exchange for problems common to all the "rational" countries at one stage or another in their development. This is but the uplifting of parochial affairs into the lap of state. It ought therefore to be instructive to learn how the state intends to deal with them.

The present New Delhi government came to power in the spring of 1971 on the slogan "*garibi hatao*—banish poverty." The unexpectedly overwhelming majority that returned Indira Gandhi was seen by many as yet another high yield of the green revolution. The implication was, however, that victory had not been given in gratitude but in high expectations, and this was lost on no one. Mrs. Gandhi had campaigned with a promise of social change. It was a promise, both her well-wishers and her critics concur, that cannot be broken, and thunderous voices have raised the cry of "last chance."

The first thrust of the green revolution has been noticeably broken. Having capitalized on the previously underexploited capacity of agriculture and having used relatively low-cost investments to augment the existing facilities, the green revolution produced a great initial surge forward. Now, however, the overextended infrastructure—land, labor, roads, transportation, marketing facilities—is bursting at the seams, and maintaining the momentum would require much greater investments.

The government nevertheless continues to uphold a dauntless posture, marked with determination. If the mood in New Delhi one or two years ago had been an ephemeral feeling that all things were possible, it has come down to earth somewhat, to a rather sturdy, if calculated, optimism, a sublime kind of faith in crisis management and the goodness of time.

The government of India recognizes agriculture, which is the full-time occupation—though not employment—of

70 percent of its 550 million people, as the very foundation of the state, requiring by far the major share of its concern. It has studied thoroughly and with considerable expertise every conceivable problem involved and has come up with a sensible scheme to resolve or attenuate every one of them.

The current five-year plan, embracing all sectors of the economy and running until March, 1974, has been built to a very large degree on the potentials of the green revolution. It envisages tremendous gains over the next few years in both agriculture and industry, which are expected to dip into the lowest strata of the population in terms of raising standards of living. As a result of the green revolution, writes Trevor Drieberg, an independent analyst of Indian affairs,

> For the first time in history, the Indian farmer is entering the market today in a big way as a buyer of consumer durables such as pedal and motor bicycles, scooters, sewing machines, transistor radios, wristwatches, electric fans, and even domestic refrigerators. All these are status symbols in the rapidly modernizing village.[24]

When the green revolution spreads throughout the countryside, he says, "Indian industry will be hard put to cope with the vast hunger for manufactured goods of all types this will create. Indeed, the hunger already exists, but the surplus money to assuage it, lies in the hands of the rural elite alone . . ."

The avowed purpose of all the schemes and strategies, however, is to provide for a more even distribution of the wealth generated by the green revolution, while broadening the base of the new technology. The government of Mrs.

Gandhi is the first to admit that this requires, above all, a retooling of the nation's social institutions, including land reform.

To alleviate the problem of unemployment, there are "crash" programs for rural works such as irrigation, afforestation, and road-building.[25] To help the small farmer, there are plans to extend agricultural credit institutions, replacing the moneylenders of the countryside, who extort up to 50—even 100—percent interest. For the landless peasant there are land reclamation and settlement schemes, as well as ways to put him to work raising livestock. To cope with the rural exodus, there is an exciting concept of polycentrism, developing India's 550,000 villages as "growth centers," bringing all the lures of the city to the countryside. There is no shortage of honest commitments to balancing the Indian diet; teaching family planning, giving "land to the tiller," capital to research, security to small farmers; constructing a streamlined agricultural infrastructure; and effecting a general transformation of all India, "leading to a more egalitarian society," as it is sometimes articulated there.

To assure that these programs are carried out as vigorously as possible, Mrs. Gandhi has established national commissions to identify priorities, refurbished government machinery, and brought to power the dynamic, popular, controversial, almost radical C. Subramaniam as her Minister of Planning. Subramaniam is sold on the need for an institutional overhaul as the crux of the problem. The archaic framework, he said recently, "will have to go in this country."[26] He believes that the dominant castes, a few leading families, or "bullies," still control much of village politics, and more important that "something of this nature has perhaps taken place at the national and, more particularly, at the State level during the two decades of democratic rule in India."

"Those in power," he said just prior to taking office, "have as a rule tended to function, by choice or unwittingly, as the spokesmen of the traditionally dominant class in Indian agriculture." [27]

Thus the question of modifying this condition would seem to be of overwhelming importance to assure that the benefits of the green revolution accrue not just to the haves but to all. T. K. Oommen, a sociologist of the University of New Delhi, believes that such change would be exceedingly difficult. He says that since "the most brilliant men" of the Indian Administration Service are members of the rural elite, in many cases the children of large landholders, little will be done against the interests of this class.[28] Subramaniam adds: "Even where they [the members of the power structure] have come from a different background they have been pressurized or misguided into not bringing about the needed changes with necessary ruthlessness or speed."

It is on the issue of land tenure, which is the most crucial factor determining the advance of the green revolution, and, as might be expected, the sorest point of the landholder-governor class, that all the schemes of the Planning Commission become blurred and confusing. All past attempts since independence have produced much on paper, but only 3.5 percent of India's total cultivated area was affected, and less was actually touched. The old feudal incubus still exists, in defiance of the substantive social changes worked by the green revolution. In many respects it is worse than before, when the practice of subsistence tenancy relegated the lease on the land to the domain of the poor, affording them at least some security. Today, under so-called commercial leasing, the landowners treat only with tenants affluent enough to make the capital investments of the green revolution. Moreover, as has been said, now that the new technology has made Indian farming highly remunerative, the owners have gone over to cultivating the best lands themselves, evicting tenants of any kind or reducing them to the status of hired hands.

Agrarian laws have abolished the hated *zamindars,* and ceilings have been placed on the size of holdings. But the same latifundists wear a different hat today, and they are deft in passing through the needle eyes of the laws. Few persons of power in India truly care to see this change, and the well-meaning handful who do, such as the new Minister of Planning, lack the required means.

Yet, without land reform, and an appropriation of some of the wealth a rationalized agriculture would yield, the programs of the Planning Commission cannot be properly funded. A tax on agricultural incomes might be a temporary alternative means of financing, but those who would have to legislate such taxes are those who would have to pay it. Drieberg says: "There is not the slightest chance that this measure, which is bound to alienate the rural elite, will be implemented, at least in the foreseeable future." [29]

The helplessness of the New Delhi government to deal with this fundamental problem, in spite of good intentions, and the out-and-out unwillingness of the individual states, to whom the right of taxation belongs, to impose agricultural income taxes are clouded with well-advertised illusions.

"There is simply not enough land to go around," according to Burra Venkatappiah, the agricultural member of the Planning Commission.[30] "If you divide the amount of land by the number who want it, you can see that this is impossible," he says, echoing the government's (and the landowners') case. Those who evade the ceiling laws must be ferreted out, he maintains, but it is not necessary to own land to enjoy a higher standard of living. "Unfortunately, the ownership of land has taken on prestige value," says the commissioner. "I do not know what can be done about this, other than to try to change this cultural value." In other words, what cannot be changed in substance requires a change in one's thinking about it, which of course does nothing to alter the fact that as long as man's life supports emerge from the soil, land is his first estate.

The myth of land shortage in India was attacked most dramatically by the left-wing parties in 1970. Under their leadership, the land-grab movement occupied only those farms that exceeded the ceiling and were owned by members of government, leading political figures, or major industries. The land-grabbers apparently sought to demonstrate that the ceilings were ineffective; that landownership was being used as a tax haven for business interests; that the plea of no surplus land for redistribution to the landless was a deliberate falsification; and that those in positions of power were the worst offenders.

They made their points emphatically, but they certainly did not prove, by selective raids on a relatively few owners, that land in India was really abundant. The indisputable data, which reveal that the national territory contains less than 1.5 acres of cultivated land per rural inhabitant and that the farm population is growing at a much faster rate than any new lands might be reclaimed, are very impressive. When matched against the 100 acres for every member of the *declining* United States farm population, it argues very strongly against the value of equitable land redistribution and, *for* population control.

It is not always pointed out, however, that Japan, which has one of the best agricultures in the world, has half as much land per rural inhabitant as India, and nearly twice the population density. The Netherlands, with perhaps *the* best agriculture in many respects, has a man-to-land ratio about one-fourth that of India. As for population growth wiping out these advantages—since India is gaining in numbers of people much more rapidly than Japan or the Netherlands—there is no controversy about the observation that an increase in well-being, which would undoubtedly accompany seriously undertaken land reforms, is a principal factor in reducing birth rates.

In India, as in most poor countries, large families are valued by the poor as a means of securing one's old age. Sons are thus appreciated more than daughters, whose status in India is scandalously low. But daughters come along in equal numbers with sons, making families, on the average, twice as large as their creators would like them to be. Security established by other means, such as by land tenure, bring about a dramatic fall in birth rates, which is what happened, for example, in Japan, and is now occurring in China.

Very often it is argued in India that redistribution of land would render farm sizes too small to be economically viable. There is some truth in this, but hardly enough to justify the present situation. The pooling of agricultural resources, *following* redistribution, would certainly suit Indian conditions well. Collectivization need not repeat Stalinist patterns, and the history of the self-governing, now quite successful cooperatives of Yugoslavia,[31] to mention one instance, can be very instructive to any nation embarking on a program of earnest reforms. There is no scarcity of solutions to the technical side of land reform; no other agrarian problem has been studied so exhaustively.

In any event, farm sizes are less important than they

used to be. The average in Japan is about 2.5 acres, and more than half the peasants cultivate smaller plots. If, in nineteenth-century Ireland, "insanely fragmented" holdings helped bring on the famine, the green revolution is technologically neutral to economies of scale. It is only weaknesses of an infrastructural nature that limit the small farmer's efficiency. Studies have found that the threshold at which poor farmers becoming willing to adopt new techniques lies not much beyond a point where the advantages to be derived are 25 percent higher than those of existing practices.[32] Where innovation promises only 5 or 10 percent gains, the benefits are obscured by inertia and real or imagined risks, not the least of which may be the furies of the evil eye. The green revolution, as we have seen, can yield advantages far in excess of 25 percent, but the advantages often do not materialize for the small farmer.

In India, the large owner can walk into almost any bank and obtain the financing necessary to convert his holdings to the new technology, which is considered a high-growth investment. The small farmer, however, must rely on the moneylender, since his ability to repay agricultural loans is in question, given the present setup. Ashok Thapar explains:

> This is because the total output of a farmer with five acres is of necessity much smaller than that of one with fifteen acres. After the small farmer has kept back what he needs for personal consumption, what he has left over for the market is often only a small part of his total crop. And since his staying power is limited, he has to sell immediately after the harvest when prices are at their lowest. The actual cash he gets is in many cases less than the amount he has borrowed to buy seeds, chemical fertilizers and other inputs.[33]

Research in one green revolution area in India (in the state of Uttar Pradesh) confirms this.[34] By 1970 half the small farmers in the districts studied had managed to go over to the new technology and increase their yields by 50 percent. The study measures to what extent the agricultural infrastructure was weighted against them. In 1969 the small farmers who were growing the new dwarf wheats were able to sell only 39 percent of their output, while farmers in the same district with fifteen acres or more sold 73 percent. The small farmers earned an average of 217 rupees per acre, which was 33 rupees less than the per-acre cost of cultivation—a net loss of more than 10 percent. This still represents an improvement as compared with small farmers who had not modernized. Since the green revolution farmer had satisfied his personal wheat needs for the year, he could grow other high-yielding crops in the coming months, have a greater marketable surplus, and pay for his labor costs and other services with his unsold surplus wheat. The large farmer, however, received a cash return for the same superwheat of 795 rupees per acre, and a net cash profit of 345 rupees per acre—or an exuberating 185 percent return on investment.

The following year, according to the study, matters improved somewhat for the small farmer. He earned a net profit of 44 rupees per acre for his crop of superwheat. Under compulsion to obtain cash as quickly as possible—in order to pay back the moneylenders—the small farmers had been forced to sell as soon as the crop was taken, when the market was glutted. Had they, like the richer farmers, been able to hold off for a few months, by which time the price for their superwheat had risen from the floor of 76 rupees per quintal to 110, their profits would have been about 50 percent higher.

The authors of this study concluded, quite irrefutably, that any development plan that does not ensure substantially higher earnings can in the long run merely result in pushing the small farmer further into indebtedness. This situation is but one example of many of the "second generation problems" of the green revolution. It is irremediable without massive institutional reconstruction of the most nation-shattering kind—the very thing India cannot yet do. In the jargon of agricultural economists the prevailing infrastructure may be said to be filled with powerful disincentives, which can bring on a regression to subsistence farming. But it does not appear likely that this can happen in India, where the pressure of population growth precludes retreat.

The hunger for land in India, for the security agrarian reforms could provide, and the resources they would release, is today greater than the hunger for food. This much the green revolution has done. But it can do nothing to appease land hunger. This is a role for men. If the role is not filled, there can be no meaningful institutional changes in India since the very condition of such change requires the same reallocation of the social power necessary to carry out land reform. Land reform, as has been said, is the first barrier. The nation that cannot remove it is reduced to merely loosening the social bedrock so that trickle-down capitalism can trickle a little faster.

It was the Homestead Act of 1862 that gave land to the American tiller, and as a consequence broke up the vast, unproductive holdings of the post-Colonial latifundists (holders of huge land tracts); it also helped to check rapid population growth in the United States. The twentieth-century land reforms of Japan, Taiwan, and Mexico, in spite of grave defects, gave those countries the high level of agriculture they command. It was no accident that the tropical technology was born and penetrated most deeply in Mexico. That it has barely touched the rest of Latin America, or at least that greatest part where 95 percent of the land is owned by 5 percent of the people, ought to be a lesson for India as she watches her green revolution grind to a halt.

True enough, there remains much room for expansion even without major reforms. The intensification of the technology on existing green revolution land can add significantly to output, although this too generates new problems with respect to the world market. In 1971 Indian farmers harvested a record 108 million tons of food grains. This was a rather astonishing 8.5 percent gain over the previous year, in which a record was also established. It was 3 million tons more than had been expected.[35]

The primary area of Indian agriculture, rice, which until now has not done as well in that country as wheat, seems ready to open a second, farther-reaching round than the success in superwheat. Capital feedback into Indian agricultural research and development has produced new, more sophisticated strains of miracle rice, which can outperform the earlier dwarf varieties. The new rice breeds are resistant to the diseases and pests that on Indian soil plagued IR-8 and its successors, and scientists have stamped the problem "solved."[36] Rice seeds can be multiplied much faster than wheat, and within a year or two the paddy fields, which are at least twice as extensive as the land given over to wheat, are expected to redouble all that the green revolution has already brought—including the problems.

This is hardly the full picture. A recent report of new research accomplishments at the Indian Agricultural Research Institute,[37] noted significant progress in high-yielding, high-protein wheat, rice, pulses, and vegetables. The pelleting of bacterial cultures, which fix free nitrogen in the soil, was announced, and this has a potential for reducing the need for inorganic fertilizer—a drain on foreign exchange for India, which must import much of its fertilizer. High-yielding, quick-ripening grapes, dwarfing the roots of fruit trees for high-efficiency management, the dry-land farming of high-yielding cotton, and a durable, sweeter-smelling, chocolate-colored rose are also being developed and have an important marketing potential.

The schemes of the Planning Commission, India's $400-million family-planning program, her highly animated export trade, and industrial growth moving toward a target of 8 percent a year, foreign investment and aid—in short, the latest World Bank model of loose-rock, trickle-down capitalist development—are bound to raise living standards for all. The government's sense of commitment to the model will undoubtedly add even more. But there is no trickle that can keep pace with the population imperative, and all who try to contest the one against the other must sooner or later concede, or be taken by the notion that some people should not have the right to live.

VI

INSIDE THE "FOURTH WORLD"

THE LATEST DOCUMENTATION of the U.S. Department of Agriculture (February, 1972) names thirty-five tropical or subtropical countries in Asia, Africa, and Latin America that have imported the new seeds.[1] It limits its definition of high-yielding varieties to the dwarf breed of wheat developed by, or derived from, Borlaug's work in Mexico and the Chandler's rice in the Philippines.

As for acreage, the USDA has knowledge of only twenty-three of these countries, that, it says, have more than 50.5 million acres sown to superwheat or miracle rice, or both. Mexico, not included in the total, has 1.6 million acres of dwarf wheat. In addition, the document gives information from which it can be concluded that China, North Vietnam, and Cuba have no less than 3.1 million acres under high-yielding rice, of both Chinese creation and the Ford-Rockefeller, Philippine strains.

This adds up to thirty-nine countries, apparently with considerably more than 55 million acres of green revolution land. From other sources, particularly the FAO, one can safely guess, however, that the number of countries and the millions of acres are substantially higher than currently estimated, and this does not include all the other high-yielding crops now being raised in the tropics.[2]

The impact of the new seeds varies from country to country, and from region to region within the countries involved. This is not the place for a site-by-site assessment of the green revolution, but a lot depends on how much headway it has made, and headway seems in some way inversely proportional to the size of the social obstacles encountered.

Thus in Mexico, where land reforms were carried out after the revolution of 1917, it has given that country, according to a Ford Foundation study, "rapid and sustained agricultural development during the last quarter of a century, increasing the availability of agricultural and livestock products per person, even in the face of explosive population growth."[3]

In Brazil, where the Minister of Agriculture recently admitted that virtually no social progress had been made since the generals' "revolution" of 1964 and that none is foreseen in the near future, the green revolution has barely gained a foothold. But even in Brazil, which is not even listed in the USDA report, the new technology, adopted by the richer farmers of the central-south region, has helped that country cut its wheat imports in half.

The pattern of unreformed land-tenure systems, wherever it appears in this "Fourth World" of green revolution countries, fixes definitively the limits of the green revolution today. This has done nothing, however, to dampen the argument that the contrary is true—that is, that the green revolution diminishes the need, or is a substitute, for reforms. The Ford Foundation report referred to above—

authored by Eduardo Venezian and William Gamble—goes still further, suggesting that Mexico's land reforms have impeded, not fostered, her "uninterrupted development in agriculture."

"The fact is," Venezian and Gamble assert, "that after so many years of revolution and reform, made by and for the peasants . . . those who have benefitted the least are precisely a majority of the farm population." [4]

This is indeed a fact, but it only shows how great is the distance between facts and how they may be interpreted. It is another fact, about which the authors did not comment, that Mexico's intensive land and resource redistribution reached the end of the line in 1940, and that ever since then the trend has been in reverse, economic concentration taking place in spite of laws and tributes to Zapata.[5] Rather than confirm Venezian and Gamble's general conclusion that private farms are more productive than the *ejidos,* which in itself is probably true, their observation about the plight of the Mexican poor more likely shows that halfhearted reforms only lift half the barrier. This concept is in any case a more useful companion on journeys through the lands of the green revolution since it appears to be the only way to explain in a general way why the new technology goes far in one country and fizzles fast in another.

The case of the Philippines shows what happens when reforms are even less than halfhearted. The Philippines, birthplace of miracle rice, has undergone two green revolution miracles in the past four years. It had been an importer of rice until 1967, when it converted to the new technology. The following year the country made headlines when it announced its first miracle: going from a rice-deficit area to self-sufficiency, and then to exporting the commodity, all in the same time period. Now, four years later, with the government seeking less publicity, the Philippines is a rice importer once again.

When *The Economist* of London learned of this, it inquired what had gone wrong. "Has miracle rice suddenly turned to chalk?" it asked rather sardonically.[6] "Are farmers producing less? Has the number of rice-consuming mouths increased so fast in four years that they have gobbled up the trebled yield of the miracle grains? Was it mice?"

"Not at all," said *The Economist,* having satisfied its curiosity. The trouble lay, it concluded, in a lack of institutional reforms, or rather, in the breakdown of quarter-hearted reforms, causing the price of rice, in spite of surpluses, to triple in three years. The government had decided to dump imported Japanese rice on the home market to depress local prices. "This was apparently worth the risk of destroying the image of the country as the pioneer of miracle rice seeds," it said; "the alternative was to let high local rice prices inflame the rural population"—the urban Filipino being already visibly angered. The outlook was hardly reassuring, for, according to the publication's correspondent, the administration responsible for reforming the country's agricultural infrastructure "has been bumbling along . . . without a friend at court with sufficient leverage to push its policies through the paper tunnels of this most contorted of all bureaucratic machines in Asia."

Almost every foreign correspondent feels that the country from which he is reporting has the worst bureaucracy, and he cannot be very far from wrong, as it is easy to prove that one is worse than the other. But a deeper descent beneath the surface of the events in the Philippines clearly shows what occurs when the green revolution gets entangled in the social net in which it is trying to unfold.

Such a descent has been made by Arthur Gaitskill, who

has spent a lifetime studying and living in underdeveloped countries, particularly in Asia. At a London University postgraduate seminar on land reform held in 1968, Gaitskill gave a paper dealing with his observations in the Philippines.[7] This document is worth reviewing, since once the matter of that country's two "miracles" has been elucidated, little more need be said here about land reforms in the other green revolution countries outside the Communist group. The Philippines has so many features in common with the others that only insignificant variations of one or another of these aspects can be found anywhere else. Indeed Gaitskill, turning to other underdeveloped countries, makes it clear that whether the nation has feudal, colonial, semicolonial, or independent origins, the case of the Philippines is more or less an example of them all.

Gaitskill begins,

> The Philippines is the only Christian country in Asia. As such, it is under heavy criticism from the Papacy in Rome as rather a poor shop window for Christian principles. A major reason for the criticism is the marked inequality between a rich minority and the poorer masses in the country. It is also the only country in Asia where this inequality derives from a Spanish inheritance, which makes the situation somewhat similar to that in Latin America.

The Spanish were driven out by the Americans, but the system of latifundism was left behind, and social power remained in the hands of the small landowning elite. An agrarian reform movement, led by the Huks, arose, but this was interrupted by World War II, when the Huks led the resistance against the Japanese while the majority of the landowners collaborated. When the Japanese went home, the landlords returned to power, and the Huks were suppressed with the help of the Americans, who themselves withdrew, giving the Philippines, that is, the landed elite, its independence.

After the Huk revolt was crushed, however, the government legislated a comprehensive land-reform law, which, according to Gaitskill, "had a remarkable combination of desirable features." The 1964 Land Reform Code, as it was called, was designed to go much beyond merely breaking up the large estates and putting a ceiling on the size of holdings. It provided for the full emancipation of the peasant from the traditional latifundist system, doing away with sharecropping and giving full ownership to the tiller. It sought to create the conditions for rapid growth and a fair distribution of income.

This unusual land-reform law, envisaging a peaceful but revolutionary transformation of the countryside, was meant to be carried out in three sensible phases, in order that the dispossessed owners might be fully compensated and the burden of change spread thin so as to forestall collapse from too much pressure on the government's weakened financial base.

The first phase was to convert the sharecroppers to leaseholders, who were to pay a modest 25 percent of the average annual net production of the three years prior to the changeover. In the second stage the leaseholders were to begin amortizing ownership. The land was to be valued in money terms; the government was to purchase it from the landlord, and the peasants would slowly reimburse the government. The final phase would take place when the tenant had repaid, at which time he would be registered as the legal owner. During the process, the full package of support services would be made available to the peasant, and there was no shortage of trained manpower ready to carry out the job.

When all the details had been elaborated, land reform in the Philippines in fact began—off to a slow start, to be sure, but that was to be expected after centuries of inquities.

Into this happy picture rushed the green revolution, with its promise of the highest production and profit. It was an uncanny coincidence of the most favorable circumstances, and chance for the soil-bound peasant to fly.

"How, then, has it all turned out?" Gaitskill asks. "In reality," he replies with the kindness of understatement, "rather slowly and disappointingly."

He attributes this to several reasons, the primary one being the government's flagging political will to enforce the land-reform law. As in India, and most underdeveloped countries, the Philippine governing elite, when not the actual landlords themselves, find more things in common with them than with sharecroppers, whose status in the Philippines is especially low.

Thus, to take a small but important example, when the inevitable arguments developed between landlord and sharecropper as to what was the three-year average yield —information needed to establish the aspiring leaseholder's rent—the disputes were referred to courts, where family connections are often above the law. The courts are presently deluged with such cases, and the landlords are not losing much time worrying about how the decisions may turn out.

As for the sharecropper, he had learned, for good reason, to be faithless. He was uncertain whether the government would support him if he ever actually became a leaseholder, not to speak of becoming an owner. He wondered, Gaitskill writes, whether the government would have the money to give him the credit he needs, whether his supplies would arrive on time, "and whether the red tape involved will make the old landlord system attractively easier, in spite of its inequalities." Still, the reforms crept forward, for a while.

The sudden full-fledging of the green revolution, however, bared the separate lines of the social strata like the rings on the stump of a newly felled oak. It provided the opportunity for the Philippines to pass quickly—without changes in land tenure—from a rice-deficit nation to self-sufficiency. As a result, according to Gaitskill, the very organization and staff that was supposed to be carrying out the land-reform law—later to be characterized by *The Economist* as the "bumbling" administration that brought on the Philippines' "two miracles"—was appropriated for the task.

The hastily put together self-sufficiency program—backed by an AID-sponsored "Operation Spread"—was given a higher priority than the reforms. This was an act, as far as the reform law was concerned, of suicide. The administrators of the self-sufficiency program, Gaitskill informs, "found it easier to get quick results by playing down the need for land reform and utilizing the existing landlords."

Further, the green revolution suddenly began to appeal to these owners. Previously they had taken little interest in agriculture, often being absentees and entrusting their holdings to an overseer. Their interest in the new technology was due not only to the immediate profits it afforded. They reasoned: if substantially higher yields were to be included in the three-year averages before the shift from sharecropping to leaseholding in the first stage of the land-reform law, they would receive a much higher rent; and in the second stage, when the cash value of their land would be established for purposes of acquisition by the government, they would gain once again. Furthermore the land-reform law had stipulated that the landowner may retain all his land if he farms it himself; so he promptly began to evict his sharecroppers and then hired them if they were so fortunate—as common laborers.

Gaitskill concludes:

> Landlords have thus become enthusiastic supporters of the production drive . . . the sharecropper . . . has lost the opportunity of converting to leasehold at the old rates of yield and gathering himself the whole benefit of the new technology. For him, the burden of rental and the ultimate cost of becoming an owner have become much higher. For the nation the opportunity of correcting social inequality through peaceful land reform has become more costly and more difficult.

This is putting it rather generously. According to a detailed study of Central Luzon by Erich Jacoby, the large owners have actually continued an earlier process of becoming still larger, with holdings concentrated in fewer and fewer hands, driving peasants from the countryside to the cities.[8]

Jacoby writes:

> The pronounced expansion of the large estates is certainly of far greater importance than are the modest agrarian reform measures hailed by political propaganda and is the true reason for the continued political and economic crises [in the Philippines]. Developments in the Philippines in fact may be considered a "reverse land distribution" * and clearly prove that agrarian

* Thailand, among others, is also going in reverse. What Ladejinsky calls "the old squeeze," whereby small owners are bought out, turned into tenants, then sharecroppers, then laborers, has reduced Thailand in a single generation from a predominantly owner-cultivator country to one where now only a minority of the peasantry owns its land.

> reform programs are without any practical effect in an environment where technical and financial assistance support an economic policy which primarily serves the interests of the privileged few.

Just north of the Philippines, resting on the Tropic of Cancer, lies a politically divided country, both sections of which have instituted land reforms that have worked, though they are very different from one another. The country of course is China.

Chiang Kai-shek, when the Kuomintang ruled the mainland, had exalted Sun Yat-sen's teachings that the fair distribution of land was the "Principle of the People's Livelihood," but he openly supported the class of landlords in its oppression of the peasants. Driven to Taiwan in 1949, he had apparently learned something from the experience, however. The peasant movement had brought Mao to power, and Chiang's first order of business on the Formosan enclave was to give land to the peasants. About 70 percent of Taiwan's peasants own their own land today.[9] This is about double what it used to be, which even then was higher than what it is today for most of non-Communist Asia. It is roughly the same proportion Mao gave to the landless before converting to the more productive system of communes. Taiwan, too, incidentally, is currently consolidating its farmlands, though in a much more conventional manner than the one that established the communes.

Land reforms have given Taiwan a very high level of agriculture. Taiwan had been using much of the new technology before it became "packaged" in the green revolution. Nearly all of its rice areas had been irrigated, fertilized, multiple-cropped, etc., and the peasants had been cultivating older high-yielding varieties developed by the

Japanese. Thus, the Ford-Rockefeller miracle rice had little to offer the Taiwanese, who are moving toward a sophisticated, diversified agriculture of the type that characterizes the developed countries. Agrarian reforms have helped raise the standard of living in Taiwan to one of the highest in the Far East, with a consequent fall in population growth. The island may be said to have been above or beyond the green revolution when it appeared, the point of it all being how vast may be the possibilities that combine the mere removal of the land-reform barrier with the new technology. Taiwan has a population density more than five times greater than that of China proper (some 1,000 persons per square mile—one of the highest in the world), and the Taiwanese are being fed rather adequately, exporting sizable surpluses. Projected on a worldwide scale the Taiwanese model alone, which leaves much to be desired, could provide the life supports for a population of 60 billion people.

The green revolution on the Chinese mainland, though no one outside yet knows exactly how far it has penetrated, appears to be proving the point. That strange country has clearly emerged from the Malthusian darkness. China has no shortage of food, although some surely eat better than others. The availability of calories and protein per person, easily calculated from the known food production figures, is more than adequate.* The same cannot be said of most underdeveloped countries, including India.

China, inhabited by nearly one-fourth of mankind, has

* Food-grain production for 1970 is estimated at 230 million tons by the FAO, and 240 million by Chou En-lai. This alone is enough to supply the annual calorie and protein requirements of considerably more people than the 750 million Chinese. In addition 20 percent of China's farmlands are given over to other crops such as vegetables, soybeans, etc. Cattle, sheep, and pigs are also important commodities.

no population problem. The striking advance China has made in food production, much of it due to the new technology, has contributed to the well-being of the Chinese, helping to reduce population growth to the low level of Japan and most developed countries.[10]

The downward trend has been augmented by the communization of agriculture, which has eliminated traditional rural needs for large families. More than 80 percent of the people live in the countryside. State welfare for the young, the sick, and the aged; productive work for youth (contributing to late marriages); and improved diets for all have done more to lower fertility rates than China's attempts at birth control (China, too, was an apparent, if temporary, victim of the population establishment's rhetoric). In any case, according to the London Institute for Strategic Studies, Western-style birth-control programs have been halted since 1966.[11] True enough, China has one of the world's largest and most advanced condom machines. It has inexpensive abortions and the latest advice about family planning (which, unlike most programs in other countries, goes hand in hand with child care). It even has experimental oral contraceptives—"the medicine of the twenty-one remembrances"—and it seems to have given up the slogan "one more mouth to feed but two more hands to work." But it works hard at lowering death rates, and with a current annual population growth rate since 1967–68 estimated by the *Far Eastern Economic Review* as having fallen to 1.1 percent,[12] China has no unemployment problem to speak of; indeed it insists there are manpower shortages in many regions.

How a single government, if not one man alone, provides food and jobs, not to mention health and education, for a quarter of the human race is a subject of much study by the rest of the world, and it explains little to suggest that the trick is turned by the barrel of the gun. Compulsions—including the barrel of the gun—exist in every society in highly differentiated forms of erudition and subtleties. How the green revolution fits into the Chinese picture has also been an issue of intensive pursuit in the past three or four years, during which time China's earlier agricultural upheavals have begun to settle and pay large returns.

As has been said, not very much is known of China's green revolution, but by piecing together the fragments of hard information, a fairly accurate reconstruction can be drawn, at least for rice, which is more than half the story of the country's crops.

The latest intelligence on rice production in China, which itself does not announce any figures, has been painstakingly estimated by a special study group of the FAO. It has concluded that China harvested a record rice crop of 104 million tons in 1971.[13] This is a jump of 12 percent in the past three years, which is particularly notable since the vast majority of China's paddy fields lie too far north to gain the full advantages of the tropical technology. What remains, about 2 million acres, is, according to the USDA,[14] now almost totally sown to dwarf strains, which, it adds, accounts for about one-quarter of the total rice output in China.

This can hardly be the case, however, since it would give a per-acre annual yield for this region of a monumental 12.5 tons, which is close to the optimum obtained for miracle rice under experimental conditions with multiple cropping. It is true that this area is known to be double-cropped, and the FAO has reported recent Chinese experiments in triple cropping,[15] but it is only barely conceivable that Chinese rice culture, in spite of remarkable advances in recent years and its long history of being highly developed, could have reached such a consistently high performance.

What seems more likely is that the green revolution lands have been extended considerably. This particular Chinese enigma is deepened, however, for in 1970 the FAO noted that "large-scale land reclamation [is] no longer being actively pursued, since the uncultivated land, although extensive, is known to be of poor quality."[16] The reason it gave is that the area classified by the Chinese as "cultivable wasteland" would be slow and costly to reclaim.

Apparently China has found a way. In 1971 the FAO's China-watchers concluded that in fact a larger area was planted to rice in 1970 than in 1969. It attributed this mainly to "wasteland reclamation and early maturing varieties which permitted an expansion of the double-cropped area."[17] Extension had taken place in five provinces, all of them straddling the thirtieth parallel, the same subtropical latitude on which lie the state of Punjab and the green revolution lands of North Africa and northern Mexico. In 1972 this expansion of Chinese rice cultivation was reported to have been developed still further, both in terms of additional acreage and "the wider adoption of more advanced farming techniques."[18]

Just as the discovery in China in the year 1000 of an early ripening rice called "Champa" had allowed it to extend its paddy cultivation northward—invigorating an expanding population on which a mighty civilization (and an empire) was built—the green revolution nearly a thousand years later is favoring a repetition of the process on a higher level.

There are few obstacles, other than those of a climatic nature, to prevent the full realization of the green revolution's potential in China. The *internal* social barriers have been virtually removed, by whatever means, and the new technology is rushing in wherever it can serve. Its limitations are externally imposed, for one thing, by the developed countries' control on the world market, to which we will refer later.

The USDA finds it a "tantalizing" [19] but unanswerable question whether the Ford-Rockefeller dwarfs have been smuggled into China and whether they have "played any role in recent Chinese developments." Peking, as usual, has said nothing, but the *Sunday Times*, of London, in a story headlined "China Samples the Rockefeller Rice," [20] has reported that IR-8 was being used in China, which had obtained the seeds for 1970 spring planting through the good, and secret, offices of Nepal and Pakistan.

It would indeed be ironic if Ford and Rockefeller money, passed through the prism of advanced research, was helping to construct the foundation of the Chinese bid for superpower status. Such is the stuff that makes the footnotes of history, but while there can be little doubt that China has tested IR-8, it is impossible that it could have multiplied the seeds to any significant extent of its requirements. China has its own brand of miracle rice, therefore, as might be expected from such a country left entirely alone and all but friendless for so many years.

On a much smaller scale, something of the same could be said about the green revolution in the tortured state of North Vietnam. In 1971 the State Planning Commission reported bumper crops based on high-yielding rice strains, most of the seeds for which apparently originating in China.[21] That year, according to Hanoi sources, the country had 1.36 million acres under high-yielding dwarf rice,[22] which is just slightly more than the amount credited to South Vietnam by Washington, which ought to know.

Some 60 percent of the north's rice areas are now under the new technology. A 1970 broadcast by Hanoi radio said that "we are not yet familiar with it,"[23] but another North Vietnamese source has declared that with the green revolution "we will be able to adopt many more valuable varieties such as Agricultural 8 and Agricultural 5, which . . . we are growing experimentally over large areas."[24] Exactly what "Agricultural 8" and "Agricultural 5" might be was left unsaid, but they readily call to mind the Ford-Rockefeller IR-8 and IR-5. IR-8 seed, according to Western reports, has been obtained by Hanoi through Hong Kong "and elsewhere."[25]

Cuba openly admits having a quarter of a million acres planted in IR-8 (as of May, 1970), which it said it got "overcoming innumerable difficulties."[26] What they were, no one who knows has yet revealed, though it seems Havana acquired two pounds of the seed in Mexico,[27] and two Cuban officials visited Chandler's rice research institute in 1969 and somehow obtained small seed samples of twenty-six experimental breeds. The USDA says that Cuba's IR-8 "evidently is doing quite well."[28]

Like China, the other two green revolution Communist countries have undergone land reforms, a continuing process for all three nations. There are no serious impediments to the spread of the green revolution in North Vietnam and Cuba, particularly if the recent conciliatory posture of their principal enemy improves. Hanoi, under peacetime conditions, should have little trouble providing for its 20 million people, and Havana may have much to gain from new research in high-yielding sugarcane.

The trouble awaits them, as it lurks for all the countries of the green revolution, in the international marketplace, where the traders of the goods so backbreakingly produced by the tropical technology come to call on the temperate-zone world.

The world's 50-odd million acres planted to superwheat and miracle rice is one-fourth the size of the croplands of the United States, and about the same area America normally has under wheat and rice. Ironically it is equal to the number of acres for which the U.S. has paid its farmers in the past three or four years to withhold from crop production to protect their position on the world market.[29] This points to the impact the green revolution has had on the international economy. But protection cannot be bought for very long, even with America's resourcefulness.

The FAO's Indicative World Plan, a costly and sophisticated exercise in futurology, foresees that by 1985 there will be not 50 million acres of the dwarf breeds but 500 million acres of green revolution land producing wheat, rice, corn, millet, sorghum, and so on.[30] This means that one-third of the world's acreage given over to grain production will be under the tropical technology, giving yields that will account for much more than one-third of the global output. With the price of grain already in steady decline, many people who think about such things have expressed alarm.

The Organization of Economic Cooperation and Development (OECD), a sort of rich man's club of the most developed countries of the non-Communist world, employs thinkers of this kind, and Montague Yudelman is one of them. He runs the OECD "Development Center," and has recently reviewed the progress of the green revolution and the effects it is having and is likely to have on the world market. "There is increasing evidence," he writes, "that the recent upsurge in production of food grains in food deficit countries . . . is leading to a dramatic change in prospects for expanding world trade in grains." [31]

He means a change for the worse. For the last 200 years or so, the people of the underdeveloped world have been coming onto this earth only to act out a wretched paradox: They live in essentially agricultural countries; yet they must import much of their food. As a result of colonial domination, through which their countries' underdevelopment began (as one writer has put it: "India in the middle of the eighteenth century was no more 'underdeveloped' than the France of Louis XV or the England of George III" [32]), their agriculture was developed primarily to satisfy the needs of the mother countries. The proconsuls of colonialism, at the expense of food crops needed by the local populations, put the accent on silk, jute, tobacco, coffee, tea, cotton, sugar, etc. They halted nascent industrialization and destroyed a primitive balance between people and resources, bringing on increases in malnutrition, famine, and disease.

By the time the green revolution began to take hold, the underdeveloped countries were buying about three-quarters of the world's rice exports (the United States being the biggest supplier) and more than half of wheat exports. For this, in 1969, they spent some $2 billion, most of it going to the richest countries.

The new technology is rapidly putting an end to this business as the countries of the "Fourth World" are one by one becoming self-sufficient in grains. India in 1970 reduced its wheat imports by 20 percent and rice by 60 percent over the previous year, when sharp cuts had also been made.[33] Imports of all agricultural products into Asia declined by 10 percent between 1967 and 1970, and in the five-year period ending in 1969, the value of agricultural exports fell by 24 percent.[34] Stockpiles of wheat and rice among some major producers have doubled and tripled in the past few years.

Thus the old colonial pattern is being broken. But the new one, which is emerging, appears worse than the one it is replacing—in the long run detrimental to all; in the short run, once again, the curse of the weak.

As the green revolution countries go over from self-sufficiency to surpluses, they are seeking outlets in the contracting world market. But they cannot compete against the big powers. For one thing, now that the market is narrowing, as Yudelman has pointed out, the OECD countries are offering "very generous repayment terms" to their customers, "terms which new exporters are unlikely to match." [35] Such transactions, multiplying swiftly, have already taken over 30 percent of the world market in rice, for example, and as a result, the underdeveloped countries' earnings from exports of this commodity declined in 1971 for the seventh consecutive year.[36]

Yudelman's conclusion is that if the green revolution countries "enter export markets at any cost, this would create further serious strains . . . It would negate the benefits which might be expected to flow from a more rational, international division of labor based on considerations of real costs of resource use. However, just as this concept implies that not all developing countries should strive to be exporters of grains, it also challenges the protectionist policies followed by many developed countries." [37]

There the cure is worse than the malady. While it is assuredly true that the big powers' self-protectionism is seriously wounding the underdeveloped countries, the "international division of labor based on . . . *real costs of resource use*" that most development economists have in mind, is an ominous carving, very much resembling in effect, if not form, the large works of the colonial past-masters.

The Asian Development Bank, which looks after the interests of the elites in several Southeast Asian countries, has worked out such a scheme for the 1970s with the help of an "Expert Group" of economists from the developed world. It is anti-self-sufficiency and has as its single "most important factor" the controlled spread of the green revolution. In its own words, "The new strategy is to export processed or semiprocessed products from farms, plantations, forests, and mines. To keep the exports competitive in the world market, *wages must be kept low.*" [38] It has not a word to say about land reforms, but it concludes, quite rightly, that there is a rising demand in the developed world for the natural resources of Cambodia, Indonesia, Laos, Malaysia, the Philippines, Singapore, Thailand, and South Vietnam. To exploit this, "a reduction in the number of new mouths to be fed" is necessary and "effective links must be forged to connect the region's abundant natural resources" with the developed countries' demands.

It is unlikely, however, that the underdeveloped countries in general can be made to submit to this late-model, "rational," big-power international division of labor, whose rationality is reminiscent of a beehive. In the end, the demands of native demographic pressure on resources must necessarily be greater than the demands of the faraway, relatively minuscule affluent. The rich, at some distant date, will have to find other means—or meanings—upon which to base their wealth. On the other hand, it seems equally unrealistic, for the time being, to imagine that the developed world will lower their protections, and, in fact, the trend has been markedly in the opposite direction, as witness the dramatic turn in American foreign economic policy of 1971.

Yudelman sees international trade in general as "one of the major issues in the Seventies," with which the OECD countries "will have to come to grips." The FAO says that the buildup of surpluses in the green revolution countries will give them a "moral claim" [39] to call for changes in the jaundiced system of international trade. But it is difficult to recall the last time a moral claim was heard. The publication *Far East Trade and Development* asks, "Can a trade war, now in the offing, be avoided?" [40] It hopes so, but it sees the protectionist tide in the United States and elsewhere running strongly. It appeals for "a new sense of belonging to a broad community," but the Manila *Chronicle* says, "Appeals to the heart are inevitably drowned in the market place." [41]

The tariff walls built by the OECD countries to keep out all others are due to be refortified in the next few years. Britain's entry into the Common Market, the dropping of preferences for certain poor countries by America, and Japan's reluctance to modify its unnecessary program of surplus rice production make the outlook for the poor countries bleak. For the *Far Eastern Economic Review* the "war" is already on: It writes:

> Greed, ignorance and cynicism are the battle cries in the current war between the world's rich and poor economies over trade and tariff concessions for developing nations. . . . the rich are determined to drop as few crumbs from their table as possible . . . The poorer nations may well be compelled to reduce their involvement in international trade to a minimum. The breaking-point will come probably over food. The agri-

> cultural upsurge in Asia has meant a serious dislocation of traditional trade relations. . . . The failure to be generous is the result of timidity among politicians who refuse to resist vested interests at home and general unawareness in the West of human costs of total, unremitting and apparently hopeless destitution. This sort of dilemma is the stuff of which revolutions are made.[42]

It is not historically true, as we have pointed out earlier, that revolutions are made of unrelieved misery alone, and there appears to be no need to be wholly pessimistic about the avarices of the affluent. It is in their interest to alleviate the rot of the underdeveloped world, and whenever they can do so, without much sacrifice to their own well-being, every effort will surely be made. Their bargaining position is mighty, however, and only the very least is usually given away; yet it has been proved for at least a generation that liberalism is the stablest form of big-power rule, albeit the most expensive.

Some things are therefore more possible than others, and the *Far Eastern Economic Review* is probably right in suggesting that the "breaking point" is food, although one cannot foretell what might happen when the point is reached. The structure of agricultural production is highly organized in every country and extremely difficult to alter. Even more so is the world system of trade in grains, which is sensitive to relatively minor changes in supply and demand.

What is happening now that the green revolution is building up surpluses and prices are falling is that farmers must be subsidized. Subsidies must either be paid to withhold production, as in the rich countries, or price supports set to encourage the shift to the new technology, as in the poor countries. Such supports have lately been fixed at levels rather above those of international prices, and this has led to the following consequences.[43]

The high prices paid to green revolution farmers mean a rise in prices for food for urban consumers, whose real incomes are therefore lowered, the poorest people in the cities suffering most. The high cost of food forces wages to go up, and a general wage increase encourages farm mechanization, displacing rural laborers, who go off to the cities. In this way unemployment increases.

When prices are high for grain, farmers stop growing unsupported crops, so grain acreage—and surpluses—expands, for a while, at the expense of other commodities. This cutback, however, when it affects so-called cash crops, such as cotton and silk, leads to a fall in export earnings, as the poor countries have fewer goods to sell abroad. Foreign exchange declines, and the country cannot buy the many manufactures produced only in the developed countries, particularly capital goods needed for industrialization, in the absence of which unemployment grows.

Moreover, whereas foreign aid used to be given in kind—the surplus wheat, for example, of the rich world—the underdeveloped countries no longer need this, while the developed countries do not wish to give much of anything else. Thus, foreign exchange, earned less easily than before, is needed not only for the goods the poor countries bought in the past, but for the agricultural inputs, such as fertilizer, pesticides, etc., to sustain their green revolution. Still further, where grains have been substituted for food crops of additional nutritional value, such as protein-rich pulses and vegetables, the peasant's diet suffers accordingly.

Grains supported at a high price also make livestock production, which theoretically could greatly benefit from surpluses (since grains are used as animal feed), an uneconomical activity. And, finally, price supports are made doubly costly when the surplus-producing country tries to enter the world market. The government is then forced to subsidize exports in order to compete on a buyer's world market, diverting its financial resources from its domestic commitments—like fulfilling a promise to "banish poverty."

Once price supports have been established, it is almost impossible to remove them; they are the crutches of a crippled world system, and to take them away is to fall. "Given the experience of OECD member countries," Yudelman has remarked, "it need hardly be emphasized that there is always a great resistance to lowering *any* prices paid to farmers." [44] In April, 1972, for example, the Indian government, in a test of strength, brought the full weight of its power and prestige against the farm lobby of the rural rich to reduce the guaranteed price paid for green revolution wheat by 5 percent. In the end, it could not even win a token, face-saving cut of one-third of 1 percent.[45] The fact is that price supports normally go up, not down.

Where the spiral staircase goes is hard to assess. In the long haul, surpluses in the rich countries have invariably brought about a *reduction* of farm acreage and a consequent shift of rural populations to the cities. But that was when there were jobs in the cities, of which in the Third World there are none, and the green revolution, pressed by population growth, must necessarily move a very long way outward before it stabilizes, much less retracts. Thus, the surpluses, until an answer is found, will continue to mount, freezing world trade in its tracks.

A long but interesting quotation seems in order—a prediction from Mexican development economist Edmundo Flores about what he calls the approaching "grievous age of fat cows," when there will be food and drink for nearly all and nearly all will not have the land, work, or money to enjoy them:

> In the next fifteen years [he writes] agricultural surplus stocks will increase and though their prices will decline steadily, no one will buy them. By then, international food grants will have come to a stop and world trade, in the midst of a grave depression, will be confined to the sale of tropical commodities to the temperate and cold regions. Since the relation between agricultural commodity prices and those of manufactured goods and equipment produced by the industrial nations will be disastrous for the agricultural countries which will lack foreign exchange, it will be impossible to effect the sizable unilateral transfers of equipment and machinery to the countries undergoing industrialization unless new and bold forms of financing are devised.
>
> The demonstration effects of progressive surplus stockpiling [i.e., the social awareness resulting from the tradition-shattering aspects of the green revolution], the paralysis of international trade, and rising unemployment will corrode the status quo . . . and sooner or later will lead to a redistribution of *productive land* so as to unload on the farmers the food surpluses and, at the same time, improve their social status.
>
> This will be followed by full employment policies in industry and modern services and by the organization of societies based on true equality. The abundance of food will permit the construction of the necessary overhead facilities, cities, schools, universities and research centers without atavistic fears of rationing and inflation.
>
> Thus, in providing the means to kill hunger, the Green Revolution will destroy many vested interests.

> It will force the reappraisal of the problem of landless peasants, of the unemployment of workers and of the alienation of the masses. And in the final analysis, it will precipitate a prodigious economic, social and political transformation in the developing countries.[46]

In this way the giant in the earth would be freed. But it is not the model uppermost in the minds of the technocrats of the world political economy, the global social impasse.

VII

AT THE COLD AND TEMPERATE CENTER

LENIN ONCE SAID, "Who pays says." Proverbs XXII, 7, is less pithy but more poetic: "The rich ruleth over the poor, and the borrower is servant to the lender." Ritual, repression, and, more important, the Galbraithian limitations imposed by conflicting interests obfuscate and to some extent erode the aphorisms of one or another man's Bible; yet the fundamental truth embodied in those mentioned here still stands tall in the present.

In the underdeveloped world, "who pays" is the developed world. In 1970 it bought almost everything the poor countries produced for export (nearly 20 percent of their combined gross national product). For this it paid more than $35 billion and, in addition, transferred to them slightly less than $15 billion in capital and technology in various forms of so-called aid. Along with what was spent in the poor countries by the tourists of the rich, this accounts for nearly all the foreign exchange and investment and technical assistance made available to the Third World for development.

For the advanced countries the $50 billion or so they pay out each year in aid and trade to "help" their poor relatives is less than a pittance, since all the money comes home again, literally and figuratively with interest. On an annual per-capita basis, for every $20 spent by the rich on the poor, the former receives more than $50 from the latter. In 1970, for example, the tropical countries were in debt to their temperate neighbors in an amount well over $50 billion. To service this obligation in terms of interest and amortization, they paid their creditors more than $5 billion. The poor countries spent nearly $40 billion that year buying the goods and services of the rich, and the private foreign investors sent back to their home countries several billion dollars of their profits—which represented a nearly 20 percent return on the $40 billion they have invested directly in the Third World.[1]

In the end, as is well known, the direction of capital and resource flow remains, as it has been for centuries, from the peripheral, tropical countries to the cold and temperate center, where less than one-quarter of the world's people consume considerably more than three-quarters of the world's goods. This is more than a small part of the reason why the "widening gap" between the per-capita incomes of the poorest and the richest nations now stands at sixty to one.

Nevertheless, for the underdeveloped countries the wealth they receive from abroad is vital, often the very essence of their existence. By 1977, according to the Pearson Report, they will be returning in service charges 120 percent of the money they get in foreign loans, at present rates, but until now, at least, aid and trade has helped them, on the average, to maintain a rate of economic growth a shade in excess of the tempo of the population explosion.

Indeed such assistance has meant to many poor-nation ruling elites the difference between occupying the national seats of power and honor and being hanged as a traitor to one or another Good Cause. In this way, however, a great part of the underdeveloped world is made less than independent.

Some call this state of affairs "imperialism," economic or otherwise. Others, struck by similarities with times bygone, use the term "neocolonialism." There are those who rebuke them, noting quite rightly that the poor countries nearly always invite more aid, more loans, more trade, and more foreign investment. But all this is sterile debate, for the two sides, as they are usually drawn, are not mutually exclusive. The question that intrigues and has meaning concerns the dependent relationships between the poor and the rich. And where does the green revolution fit in?

It is a rare occasion when nations or groups of nations admit to interfering in the internal affairs of others. And it is only slightly more frequent that the offended parties acknowledge such intrusions in public. Without pride and pretensions there can be no diplomacy. Undoubtedly the longest confession of this kind was recorded on September 26, 1960. That was the day Fidel Castro went before the United Nations and spoke for eight hours on how Washington had twisted the Cuban arm for half a century. Someday he might care to reveal the style favored by Moscow.

At the other end of the spectrum we have a recent and novel suggestion from Gunnar Myrdal, the indefatigable critic of the developed countries' treatment of the Third World. He would like to see the rich countries redesign their interference. "Why," he asks, "should we always misuse power, or at least shy away from using it for the good?" [2] In other words, the rich countries should tell the poor,

Myrdal says, "We would like to help you by providing you with the new seeds [of the green revolution] and creating the conditions for its application. But if you don't want to create a greater gap between rich and poor and more misery for the masses, you must carry out land reforms."

This is the "vision" Myrdal has for the future. But, on close examination, using power for "good," as Myrdal himself has clarified, can never be very much different from using power for "bad," as long as those in possession of power continue to write the definitions of terms. This in fact is precisely the event, and one can therefore imagine that much power is already being used for "good."

The World Bank, for example, which in 1970 sent more than $2 billion to the Third World, tries always to use its powers of interference "positively." The bank hardly ever says so, but at a conference on "effective aid" its attitude was made known. According to the proceedings of the conference, "The general point that providing aid necessarily involved intervention was accepted by most people. The further implication that donor countries had a responsibility to ensure that the intervention was positive and not negative, was supported in particular by the representative of the World Bank. . . . Although at first the Bank's intervention might have been painful, it was becoming more and more welcome. . . . It was important to realize how far the process had already gone." [3]

That was in 1966. By now the painful, then welcome, dynamic presumably has gone even further, though the order in some cases at least seems to have been reversed. Take Ceylon, for example, where the bank's "ubiquitous and exacting counselors," [4] to use the bitter words of the *Far Eastern Economic Review*, convinced the government to create a "climate of confidence" for foreign investors.

"How would this climate of confidence be created?" the review asks. "By slashing all things extravagant—social welfare expenditure, education, health." That this led to a Maoist uprising the following year was hardly appreciated, as has been the World Bank's demonstrable ability to influence private banking houses to cease lending to countries on its "blacklist."

One of the principal objectives of the bank's interference was elucidated in the "World Bank Report," a study prepared by a group of left-wing Scandinavian scholars. They concluded that the bank's lending was linked closely to private investment, and its policy was "to get the underdeveloped countries to design their economies and societies in such a way that they can be most efficiently exploited by the great powers." [5]

Not everyone would say it in quite that way, and in any case the interventions of the World Bank are hardly unique. Julius Nyerere, the president of Tanzania, gave the general picture in simple language, a statement remarkable in the way it breaks the *omertà* among nations:

> Sometimes the rich countries say "We've got the money so when we pull the strings, Julius, you open your mouth and jump." . . . We are not unfriendly to countries who give us aid, and we are not inflexible. There is no reason to condemn countries who help us, and sometimes when we disagree with their policies, I judge it best to keep my mouth shut.
>
> But neo-colonialism is a very real danger. It is an inevitable disease of capitalism. Unfortunately it does not only afflict capitalist countries. There are some supposedly socialist countries who also try to use their wealth to gain power and influence over the affairs of poorer countries.[6]

The rich countries, which possess, buy, or appropriate the resources needed by the poor for development, exercise their controls through many institutions. The agencies of the temperate-zone governments are deployed throughout the world. They collect the data required for decisions about which nations may be worthy of their support and what the priorities ought to be. The United Nations "family," as it refers to itself and its specialized organizations, disburses technical assistance for development projects of which it approves. Treaties among the nations of wealth determine the conditions of world trade. The World Bank group—sometimes considered part of the "family"—and other development banks finance the plans of those Third World governments that conform to standards the banks impose. The 300 or so "multinational" corporations (most in fact are American), each of which have assets far in excess of the majority of underdeveloped countries and as a group control one-fourth of the world's production of commodities,[7] choose the countries and set the terms for the movement of their capital and technology. Private foundations and voluntary organizations spend their money in the poor nations to advance their particular aims. Finally, the universities of the developed world, which have a monopoly on the most sophisticated forms of knowledge production, lend their professors to whomever they—or those who finance their programs—desire.

Some never cease to argue that, given the inheritance of history, this condition can exist no other way, at least in our time. Without doubt they are as near to the truth as the ink on the page is to the paper. What is important is to recognize its existence, for there are others who seek to deny it, or nurse dangerous illusions that it can be perfected. But it has often been the case that whoever attempts to reform these institutions merely finds himself, in the most successful circumstances, seated at the wheels of control picking and choosing in the style of those he displaced. It is a high-risk venture to tamper with big-power institutions, and even Lincoln Steffens, who had visited the "future" and found that "it works," once said that after the reformers and crusaders get done with you, you long for the old bosses. It seems fair enough that as long as the bizarre social fragments called nations cannot be pieced together homogenously, each rich country must look after its own. No one else will. Philanthropy is dead, or lies very low.

Thus it appears that the policy of AID, according to its own documents, is to exert "influence," "persuasion," and "leverage" to achieve its aims.

> Leverage [it explains] goes beyond influence and persuasion to condition aid, explicitly or implicitly, on specified host country action. Leverage may be positive or negative; aid may be withheld unless certain conditions are satisfied, or additional aid may be made available if the economic performance of the host country achieves specified standards.[8]

If a poor country's "overall performance" is "good" it is rewarded, says AID, "by generous aid allocations," not only to encourage "continued good performance" but also to induce other poor countries "to improve their policies."

Similarly, it is nothing short of reasonable, by present standards, when multinational corporations seek to protect by *Diktat* the billions of dollars they invest in underdeveloped and often unstable lands. As economist Robert Heilbroner has pointed out, there is another side to the story that only stresses the ability of the multinationals "to drive hard bargains, to win strategic geographic positions, and to exercise a powerful voice in the economic policy of the countries in which they deign to operate." For even if they do send home more profits than the capital they introduce, he says, "they are also hostages within the nations in which they have settled."[9] From one moment to the next, the knife of nationalization is at their throats. It may be used by governments and rebels of almost any political persuasion, from those who pursue the elusive "higher morality" to others who are simply vulgar bandits, and though in America the Hickenlooper Amendment punishes (by cutting off U.S. aid) nationalizers who fail to "take appropriate steps," the plunge is often taken.

It is even understandable, though harder to defend, when universities put up their knowledge of how they think the Third World can be controlled from the temperate center for sale to the highest respectable bidder, usually the foundations, the State Department, AID, the CIA, and the Pentagon. The latter's Project Camelot, when unmasked in 1965, showed how deeply social scientists were involved in Latin American counterinsurgency programs. Since then anthropologists have gone "on the warpath" for the same cause in Southeast Asia, as American sociologists, political scientists, demographers, ecologists, etc., have in Africa.[12] The discredited Project Camelot has been replaced by the far more sophisticated Project Cambridge, and the sponsor has remained the same. Project Cambridge is the costly computerization of the studies of behavioral science on such things as "stability and disorder" in poor countries. The aim is to reduce decision-making processes from months to hours, with regard to, say, when to apply influence, persuasion, or leverage. Project Cambridge envisages that sometimes less gentle forms of leverage may be required. The *New Scientist* writes,

> If the techniques to be developed by Project Cambridge were available now, the military could . . . build a model describing what makes a village friendly or unfriendly, and then try to predict the allegiance of villages on which less data (possibly just aerial photographs) was available. The model could also be used to better understand what sorts of economic, social, military, and political action are most effective in gaining the support of the people.[13]

Some intellectuals wax furious at such research on the underdeveloped world. At the 1968 convention of the American Sociological Association, Martin Nicolaus asked,

> What if the machinery were reversed? What if the habits, problems, secrets and unconscious motivations of the wealthy and powerful were daily scrutinized by a thousand systematic researchers, were hourly pried into, analyzed and cross referenced, tabulated and published in a hundred inexpensive mass circulation journals and written so that even the fifteen-year-old school dropout could understand it and predict the actions of his landlord, manipulate and control him? [14]

But universities and private foundations are only national institutions, functions of the nation-state, and the head of Project Cambridge, MIT's Douwe Yntema, has the answer to Professor Nicolaus's interrogative lament. "As a scientist," he said recently, when asked if the implications of his work disturbed him, "I am working on the faith that advances of scientific knowledge will be used for the benefit of mankind."[15]

It was to trust less to faith and the goodness of the rich countries that a serious effort has been undertaken by the less rich and the poor to internationalize development aid. Seven major reports and commissions studying the problem have in the past two years called for a significant increase in so-called multilateral aid—that is, that capital and technical assistance ought more and more to be channeled through the United Nations "family," the World Bank group, and international organizations in general, which, it is very often said, have no ax to grind.

The World Bank group, for example, claims that "it has no political, commercial or other nondevelopmental objectives to distract it,"[16] although the USDA sees the international banks as "absolutely essential" to the "large, prosperous, and growing market" for America's annual $6.1 billion in agricultural exports (because the banks help maintain "a stable system of international payments and economic growth for Free World nations").[17]

Some people, such as George Ball and Neil H. Jacoby,[18] see the multinational corporation as the future hope for the development of mankind. They envisage a sort of *Pax Mercatura,* with the "cosmocorp," as Ball calls it, the embryo of a supranational global order dominated by the "impersonal," "apolitical" interests of world businessmen rather than the narrow passions of nations. Others, perhaps because they would not care to be ruled by IBM, Ford, GM, Standard Oil, and Coca-Cola, are less sanguine. Internationalized, "apolitical," multilateral *aid,* however, has few critics and many supporters, including Richard Nixon.

Although in 1970 *The Economist* found as uncoordinated as ever the aid programs of individual countries ("where competing fairy angels are stumbling over each other's wands"), the sentiment, if not the substance, of aid-giving seems to be shifting multilaterally. Presently only about 14 percent of the OECD rich countries' aid goes through the international organizations, and no one foresees its ever getting much above the 20 percent that was recommended by the Pearson Commission. But the influence role of the internationals is much larger than the figures suggest because of an imagined relative untouchability and their good offices granting easy access to the poor countries' trust. The truth is, however, that the multilateral agencies are more and more dominated by the interests of the rich countries.

We have already seen that the World Bank admits to using leverage, and in an earlier chapter we have the words of the bank's president, Robert McNamara, indicating that the ultimate purpose of its pressure is to create for the whole world the *same* justice, compassion, morality, and sharing of the wealth that prevails in "our own national societies." Teresa Hayter, a young scholar who had the courage to publish her unexpected discoveries about the World Bank—in a study that the bank paid her to undertake and then sought to suppress—clarifies what McNamara means by the word *same.*

The bank group, and other such agencies, she says, "cannot accept changes in developing countries which might endanger existing patterns of international trade, foreign private investment, the regular servicing and repayment of debts, and other more or less general concerns of the capitalist developed or creditor countries. There is a strong emphasis in the agencies' policies and demands on the principles of free enterprise, on reliance on market mechanisms, and on the respect of private property, domestic and especially foreign." [19]

The need for change, she says, is to some extent acknowledged—"but the first priority is stability." The typical recipients of aid are nonrepresentative governments more interested, like Brazil, for one, in economic growth for a few rather than raising living standards for the many. The international banks, like all banks, are simply more concerned with one's ability to repay the loans they approve than with anything else. That some people find this surprising is a cause for lament, since what makes the banks an insidious instrument for perpetuating the status quo is their license to use the rhetoric of development to nurture public confidence in them as agencies for social change and thus enhance their powers of influence.

As Hayter points out, the banks care little about land reform and "tend actually to discourage it" [20] because of its inherent boat-rocking nature. While the latest annual report of the World Bank [21] boasts of how it has sharply increased its financial support of the green revolution (to build rural infrastructure), not a single word is said about land reform.

So much for the World Bank and affiliated and nonaffiliated development banks. In the end, most of the banking done for the Third World is handled by the old-line houses in New York and London, and the Bahnhofstrasse in Zurich, and many of them are performing the same functions as they were when they handled the business of the colonial era. In any event, the actual credit of the development banks in the poor countries may be higher than that of the individual rich countries, but it is not nearly as sturdy as that of the United Nations "family," with its system of one-man-one-vote (the World Bank has weighted voting, with the United States in exchange for being the biggest contributor receiving 25 percent of the bank's voting power, not much less than the combined voting power of all the underdeveloped countries).

Almost everyone is sold on the United Nations, which is really the only voice the underdeveloped countries have in the developed world. The United Nations and its "family" of specialized agencies never rest in arguing the case for development, for more aid, trade, and social justice; and, though it is very often pressured by the banks and rudely threatened—and punished—by the big powers, the UN, like the Church, remains unshakably committed to egalitarianism, the well-being of the downtrodden, and a Talmudic elaboration of the "inalienable" rights of man.

But any serious examination of what the United Nations family does, as opposed to what it says or what it symbolizes, cannot escape the conclusion that it is but another long arm of the world political economy.

The United States, like Togo, Trinidad, and the minuscule Maldive Islands, may have only one statutory vote in the United Nations, but the sultan of the Maldivians cannot suddenly cripple any UN agency of his choosing, as the United States did when, in violation of international law, it withheld its share of the budget (one-fourth of the total) of the International Labor Organization. The ILO's offense to American sensibilities was that it had appointed a Russian as one of its five assistant directors. The representative of Zambia can sloganize in the General Assembly, but he cannot warn the head of the FAO, as the United States and Great Britain more than once have done, that if the organization becomes "too political" (placing emphasis on land reforms and the need for power structure changes), it would be virtually put out of business.[22]

But threats are the rare exception. The "family" almost always knows what it can and cannot do. Says the FAO:

"Governments which provide the resources for the international organizations quite clearly have to have the last word."[23] To help ensure that this rule is maintained, the FBI, by the authority of Executive Order 10422, certifies and approves *every* American who goes to work for the "family," and the quota of U.S. nationals in the UN, as might be surmised about the country that is by far the biggest financial contributor, is rather large. One need not labor very long in the halls of the United Nations to sense the American influence and, even more so, the supremacy of the interests of the developed world in general. This overwhelming sensation normally obviates the need for tough talk from the big powers.

The general effect of this situation is that United Nations aid, normally technical assistance, has failed in its stated objectives of improving social conditions in the poor countries. Few, including the "family" itself, would deny this, and in one recent analysis of the shortcomings of UN technical assistance, the reasons were clearly stated: Technical assistance, writes Erich Jacoby, former head of the FAO's land reform department, "concentrated from the very beginning on . . . development of the natural resources which almost everywhere are owned, or at least controlled, by a few powerful groups."[24] This entails the preservation of the existing social order, which, says Jacoby, "has not only defeated the very purpose of Technical Assistance, but has frequently even reduced the share of the bulk of the people in the national income. . . . Technical Assistance has developed into yet another powerful external force . . ."

No agency of the "family" better typifies some of the functions of the UN in the underdeveloped world than the FAO. Because it deals with the fundamental aspects of life support, the FAO has managed more than twice as many UN aid projects as the next largest "family" development agency (the UN itself), and almost 40 percent of all the projects combined, which by 1971 had cost $3.2 billion. The FAO is beyond reproach as an invaluable primary source of information about world agriculture. It is the operative side of the organization—now along with others in the "family" being called into question within the agencies themselves—that requires some review and internal reexamination.

A postwar creation primarily of the big powers, the FAO of its own volition has gone on to strengthen its ties with the interests of the developed world, forging links, for example, with the World Bank and the multinational corporations, and in the process has grown to two hundred times its original size. "The criticism levelled at the FAO and the UN specialized agencies and others," a senior official of the organization said recently, "was that they all have their own separate empires, and, unfortunately, to some extent it is true. There is a great deal yet to be done."[25]

An illustration of one latter-day role taken on by the FAO is the appropriately named "FAO-Industry Cooperative Program," in which the organization acts in the Third World for a hand-picked group of cosmocorps, such as Ford, Unilever, Shell, General Mills, International Harvester, Ciba, and about seventy-five others, including one or two from some "anti-imperialist" Communist countries.

Standards for admission into the program "are very strict,"[26] says the FAO, which is understandable since members are given access to privileged information on forthcoming investment possibilities in the poor countries. According to one member of the club, "We understand the suspicions of developing countries which fear exploitation by business firms of countries which once dominated them. FAO can be of assistance in helping to bridge the gap of suspicion." [27]

The FAO claims to be playing the role of an "honest broker," to provide "a service informing industry of investment opportunities" and to help Third World governments "make contacts with foreign enterprises." But in June, 1970, it became slightly more difficult for the FAO to maintain its ingenuous posture when six large private banks,[28] including the Chase Manhattan of New York and Barclay's of London, formed a banking group to advise the FAO as to which of its agricultural programs might be most "promising." [28] It is not probable that agrarian reform and the expropriation of the landed establishment in the underdeveloped world will in these circumstances be given the priority they deserve.

On the other hand, the banks, the multinationals, the big powers, the poor countries' elites, and the time-servers of all may be expected to approve the FAO's comprehensive plans for the green revolution.

The multinationals would like to sell more pesticides, chemicals, and combines to the poor countries; the banks are eager to finance agricultural infrastructure; the oligarchies are hoping that the green revolution and an improved infrastructure will somehow diminish the need for reforms; the governments intend to smooth the way for all; but the FAO must view the matter in all its dimensions, and as it controls many of the institutions that shape what men think about food and agriculture, its influence on the green revolution is immense.

The FAO very early recognized the potential of the new technology and, as has been noted earlier, integrated the green revolution as a "spearhead" for its Indicative World

Plan, elevating the spread of the new seeds as first among the many things it hoped to do. Going much beyond this, on March 1, 1971, the FAO issued an "in-the-family" memorandum [29] of some 10,000 words, which was signed by the director general of the organization and called a "comprehensive paper" on the green revolution. Later in the year it was adopted almost word for word and endorsed in a resolution of the United Nations Economic and Social Council.[30] An analysis of this document gives the model by which it is possible to project the future of the green revolution, at least as it is envisaged by the rich for the poor. It is a model in which a role has been carved out for everyone with power and status, one which, when followed—and there is no apparent reason why it cannot be pursued for a while—is all but guaranteed to help keep the world political economy running more or less changelessly for yet another unknown period of years.

The FAO memorandum is the outcome of "intensive discussions" held in 1970 and 1971 by the agencies of the UN "family" in order to work out a "common strategy" on the green revolution in their dealings with one another and the outside world.

Agriculture, says the document, is entering a highly dynamic phase in the poor countries. There are few historical precedents for this phenomenon, it goes on, and "surprisingly few empirically based facts, particularly on the social and economic impact of the 'Green Revolution.'" There is therefore a vacuum for the "family" to fill in order to serve as "a guide to planners and policy-makers." Further, an "urgent need" exists for research on social problems created by the green revolution and for "careful monitoring" of the economic side of the new technology.

The memorandum then proceeds to identify fourteen

"Areas for Cooperative Action." These include all of the subjects we have already discussed, such as population control, ecology, plant research, technology, nutrition, trade, aid, planning, unemployment, and social effects in general. In each category roles are proposed for various members of the "family" (particularly FAO, UN, UNICEF, UNESCO, ILO, UNCTAD, and WHO), as well as for other international organizations, for example, the OECD, the World Bank group, and other development banks, and finally, for unspecified private foundations, multinational corporations, and governments.

For the most part, the document seems to suggest that the wisest path of pursuit would be that of business as usual, the objective being the steady integration of the green revolution into the "system." Thus no radical action is proposed, and in the field of ecology it warns against "panicky short-term palliatives such as outright banning of DDT which can only set back developmental efforts without touching the real core of the overall pollution problem."[31]

What is generally needed, the paper says, is more population control ("this will need to be stepped up"),[32] more research, more technology, more trade and aid, and many, many more studies of the poor. To achieve these goals, and to make an overall effort to fill in the "gaps" engendered by the green revolution, greater coordination among the entities of power is essential.

This is the voice of the most enlightened members of the international community of big power instructing themselves on how to seize the time. Like any revolution, the document says, the green revolution could lead to social upheavals and "change"—a word it does not define but apparently views with some measure of alarm, for it continues: "Such harmful effects could be mitigated if means could be found to channel its benefits towards long-term goals [of social progress] . . . and not merely to immediate economic gains and individual profit maximization."[33]

It is not clear what the means might be, but the memorandum does indicates that "a major restraint lies also in outmoded land tenure systems."[34] It proposes to give "high priority" to *study* the problem,[35] neglecting to add that the titles alone of the studies the FAO has made on land reform make a book that is two inches thick.[36]

Although the FAO memorandum treats the green revolution as an unexpected development that nevertheless can be more or less dealt with by the "family" and other existing international and national machinery employed in the processing of such things—provided the system is alert and prepared—the document does project the formation of a few new institutions, one or two of which have ambiguous, if not preoccupying, implications.

One of these would be a computerized "Agricultural Research Intelligence Service,"[37] collecting data worldwide in order to centralize the management of research. In other words, the determination of what is to be researched would be decided by the traditional conservationists of the status quo. Who else ought to make such decisions is not exactly certain, and this is more or less as matters stand today, but through centralization and computerization, control over tropical technologies would be more secure. That is why this particular project promises "to fill outstanding essential gaps"—a phrase that has no grammatical sense but certainly conveys an uneasy feeling in this context, since one man's gap is often another's opportunity.

Finally, and most thought-provoking, are the proposals made for social research.[38] The document finds that policy-makers are inadequately supported by a "true appraisal" of the economic and social effects of the green revolution. Especially needed, it says, are studies that indicate what set of national or supranational policies might, when harmonized, act to increase the poor countries' "absorptive capacity" for social unrest, notably unrest arising from the real threat of massive unemployment.

In summary, what is being proposed is new forms and higher efficiencies of controls over knowledge, people, and their institutions in order that "more rational judgments" be made concerning "the strategy" for the green revolution. With such strategies, the "family" and its friends in the cold and temperate zones hope, in the document's words, to bring about a new "quality of life" in the tropical countries of the world.

What this might be, and how it will all turn out, no one can say. The "family" is not noted for its efficiency; the rich countries are even less celebrated for their magnanimity, and it is a mistake to think that people cannot alter the quality of their lives on their own, to their own measure, in spite of big power standing like a cop on every corner. Whenever in the past they have tried to do so, however, the whistle has always been blown, and strife has ensued.

VIII

THE CHALLENGE

THE GREEN REVOLUTION, generated by the pressures of population growth and resisted by the global social impasse is precipitating a new era of disquietude. By providing the means with which nations paralyzed by the status quo can produce more food than people, the green revolution has secured the momentum of rapid population growth. By urging forth proposed solutions—to the questions it is helping to create—which at best envisage only more of what is already being done, the further intensification of these problems seems assured for some years to come.

This is a crisis. The difficulties caused by the green revolution—which are quite different from its *potential*—are fundamental parts of what McNamara calls "a much wider social and political crisis which grows deeper with each decade and threatens to round off this century with years of unrest and turbulence: a 'time of troubles' during which the forces of historical change threaten to disintegrate our frail twentieth century society."[1]

The president of the World Bank would appear to be

quite correct when he warns his Board of Governors that "we cannot divert these forces." The overwhelming majority who "jostle behind" the affluent, he says, "certainly have no intention of renouncing or missing the wealth and prosperity, above all, the power locked up in modern technology." He is right to quote Lester Pearson's conviction that "a planet cannot, any more than a country, survive half-slave, half-free, half-engulfed in misery, half-careening along towards the supposed joys of almost unlimited consumption." [2] But McNamara is candid. "The world is already allotted," he says.[3] The peasants, in spite of the green revolution, can have little hope, for the land is "overcrowded"; it is "occupied by the nineteenth century modernizers," and in the end the new technology drives the peasants from the soil to the cities.

"So the cities fill up," McNamara continues, "and urban unemployment steadily grows. . . . The 'marginal' men, the wretched strugglers for survival on the fringes of farm and city, may already number more than half a billion. By 1980 they will surpass a billion, by 1990 two billion. Can we imagine any human order surviving with so gross a mass of misery piling up at its base?" [4]

It is not misery, as has been said, that adumbrates the "time of troubles"; rather, it is the facility with which parties and movements can politicize discontent under conditions of high population density and uprootedness. But it is important to dwell on McNamara's analysis and his proposed solutions in order to understand the nature of the crisis, and the irreducible forces that warrant its growth and unhappy endurance.

The McNamara formula for narrowing the "widening gap and preventing lethal revolution" is as follows: more rapid economic growth, population control, rural and urban "renewal," "fuller" employment, economic and social research, a doubling of governmental foreign aid, and the fostering of an international "sense of community." [5]

Nothing is said about the one outstanding basic issue: the need for land reform and the disenfranchisement of the oligarchs and their little men. In the choking mass of proposals on how the rich might help the poor, the scarcity of a word in behalf of such adjustments is conspicuous. On the contrary, just as the population controllers are reaching a narrow consensus, so, too, are the big-power donors consolidating their models for aid on their harsh terms. When this effort matures, it may very well resemble Neil H. Jacoby's plan called "The Progress of Peoples."

Neil Jacoby's influence in the formulation of the rich countries' policies toward the underdeveloped world is large. He was a member of President Eisenhower's Council of Economic Advisers, a leader of OECD missions to India and Laos, and Washington's evaluator of U.S. aid to Taiwan. He is also a self-proclaimed believer in a fundamental mission of the multinational corporations, which would bring lasting peace to the world and "unity to mankind." [6] Discovering a need for a new theory and new policies for developing the Third World, he recently undertook its construction and published it at the Center for the Study of Democratic Institutions.

Of the ten "policy proposals" advanced, the four most significant were as follows (the emphasis is added):

> Adoption by less developed countries of population policies that will foster long-term development should be made *a condition of eligibility* for external assistance.
>
> All assistance to develop social infrastructure and human resources should be administered by the Inter-

national Development Association [of the *World Bank*] and other multilateral agencies, thus "depoliticizing" two thirds to three quarters of all aid.

All assistance to develop agriculture or industrial enterprises should be extended *unilaterally*, leaving an important role for both socialist and private enterprise nations.

Aid should be allocated among developing countries in proportion to the *effectiveness of its use* by recipients, and this should be measured in each country.[7]

As Denis Goulet has said, the Jacoby program may be regarded "as structurally paternalistic, inspired by a desire on the part of the rich world to domesticate the poor nation's development efforts."[8] In other words, it is a plan by which the developed capitalist and Communist countries, not to mention the cosmocorps of both, can reinforce their respective spheres of influence with all the moats, drawbridges, and parapets built to last a thousand years. Much of this plan is already in action. What is missing is the scale, coordination, simplification, and cold efficiency Jacoby suggests. As we have seen, this process, too, is well under way.

At the other extreme, the case for the dismantling of the social impasse has long ago been consigned to the writers of hortatory prose, romantic revolutionaries, and zealot know-it-alls. To argue from their dank corner is to risk discredit and abuse, to say the least. But it is rather difficult to sully the works of a senior man such as T. Lynn Smith, the dean of American rural sociologists. In 1971 he stated that after a half-century of study he had arrived at the firm conviction that the classic type of land tenure still prevalent in much of the underdeveloped world was a "dead weight," which "society should shun as it would the plague."[9] Since the beginning of history, latifundism of itself has doomed the bulk of mankind to an everlasting, servile, "creature-like existence," chained and collared by poverty, oppressive ignorance, physical decadence, and utter dependence on all things worthy of opprobrium.

Smith, in an extraordinary, brief summation of the results of his life's work, says he first became aware of this dilemma as a boy growing up in southern Colorado. The son of a rancher, he was struck by the great divide between the few who possessed the land and the many who sold their sinew to the owners for their daily bread. They were perpetually degraded by a life in which they sought to please their masters when the eyes of the overseer was upon them but in reality did as little work as they possibly could. Seeking the origins of this wretched condition, he has pursued the problem ever since, passing much of his lifetime in the Deep South and in rural Latin America.

"I am fully convinced," he says, "that the most important factor in the well-being of those who live from agricultural and pastoral activities . . . is the degree to which the ownership and control of the land is vested in those who work upon it . . ."[10] Wherever latifundism has survived, Smith writes, the landless have remained half-slave, and little has changed for the better, and much for the worse.

So it has been for thousands of years; so it must be for many more. The destinies of the haves and have-nots were drawn a long time ago, when the hunters came to the village to stay. Today their descendants in the big-power capitals, multinational board rooms, and international councils are still performing the ancient functions of reinforcing their institutions and thereby their rule.

But an historically new element has been introduced. People are multiplying faster than the builders can repair the morbid fortifications that have hitherto contained them. More important, in the green revolution these superior numbers of human beings have been given the means by which they can stay alive long enough to multiply again. If the process continues unchecked, the fortresses must fall. What may rise on their remains, no one can possibly tell.

Giordano Bruno thought that the discoveries of Copernicus might expel the "triumphant beast" of oppressive rule and liberate the soul of man. It did no such thing, of course, but it did give power to science and technology, which was the strength of the bourgeoisie, and the bourgeoisie, in its triumph, buried the feudal era. Karl Marx believed that from the womb of feudalism's capitalist replacement would come a Messianic proletariat, which would put an end to the "last antagonistic form" of society and bring justice to the world. This was a faith that is going the way of Manicheanism, but bourgeois capitalist production most assuredly has developed the powers by which it too may be replaced, although it is no longer hard to imagine advanced societies more disagreeable than our own.

Herein lies the challenge of the green revolution and all it implies. The policy of treating the world's ills with ever more massive doses of patent medicines in use since ancient times may very well precipitate the fifteen-year sequence of events leading to the grievous age forecast by Edmundo Flores: an astronomical buildup of food surpluses, world economic recession, unemployment of gargantuan proportions, and rural migrants packing the poor countries' cities twice as densely as today. Hundreds of millions of uprooted men and women, without land, without jobs, without money, living next door to plenty, will be unable to feed their children, their old, their sick, and themselves. The medieval proverb, "City air breathes free," will take on a new meaning as the cry for political revolution knells loud in the shantytowns.

In the rich countries, the prospects for alleviating poverty will appear more dismal than ever, and with the poor populations expanding without respite, the temptation to increase the doses of "aid" to the lethal point may grow overwhelming. The nastiest plans to raise substantially the death rates of the poor and to force their sterilization—proposals of the kind only hinted at today (except by the Ehrlichs and other neo-Malthusian advance men) *—will perhaps be made to appear as the best and most final solutions of all. They, one expects, will be written (as they already are) in the language of Justice and the Good Cause, and many who yearn for peace may give them full support. But such solutions have a way of being rather less final than they are thought to be and in the end the conflagration, the slaughter, and the Reign of Terror may be inescapable.

To all who seek a less apocalyptic transition through the "time of troubles"; to all who have a stake in the reconstruction of divided mankind and the reorganization of the social system built on human relationships of equality and cooperation, not on a policy of *laissez exploiter*—in short, to all who see no cause to fear but rather to welcome the giant in the earth—the challenge of the green revolution is theirs to uphold. Nevertheless, it is extremely difficult

* Some people, presumably myself included, need not worry about exercising restraint in criticizing this group. Ehrlich says such criticism from "certain segments of our society . . . is a compliment." In any event, he himself confesses that at least some of his solutions are "callous" and employ coercion. "Coercion? Perhaps, but coercion in a good cause." (Ehrlich, *Population Bomb,* pp. 161, 166.)

to conceive of how individuals or groups can effectively alter the course being pursued by the big-power political economy. The oppression of the poor is not a one-word issue like Racism, Vietnam, or the Bomb, which can harness the scarce powers citizens have before the established order. Moreover the mystification of the population explosion, ecology, and resource use, which is encouraged by vested interests, impedes all attempts at undistorted perspectives. It seems fair to say that unfortunately large numbers of well-intentioned people inside the rich countries are already convinced that population growth is a total evil, that the environment cannot support much more human life than exists today, that natural resources are rapidly running out, that technology must mean plunder, and that poverty and famine were, are, and ever will be a natural condition of man.

If men are the social products of their institutions, it stands to reason that only in rare instances will the creation be endowed with powers to change its creator. No durable culture can ever be more generous. Social systems are remade far less by individuals than by an insufficiency of maintenance energy; and it is at the appearance of this failing that the "time of troubles" invariably begins. Only founders of great religions and the discoverers of monumental principles, when favored by an extraordinary coincidence of circumstance, have altered the course of history. The rest of us can only hope to influence a circumstance. Each man and woman must grapple with his own mind and perhaps at some point, in association with others, to determine what he can and cannot do.

Such an undertaking was attempted in the summer of 1970 at a conference held at the Hague, which had some rather unusual aspects, most of which were unintended.

Like most nontechnical international meetings, the FAO's "Second World Food Congress" was prepared as an effort in public opinion formation, in this case for the purpose of prestige-building and publicizing the programs distinguishing the organization's latest director general, Addeke Boerma. To avoid a repetition of the dreary and inconsequential first world food congress, convened in 1963 by the previous director general, the FAO decided to invite not the formal representatives of various governments and groups but "private individuals" from countries throughout the world, thus allowing for more freedom of expression, and constituting a well-publicized "first" for a United Nations organization.

Hitherto public participation in FAO meetings had been characterized, to use the qualification of the Hague conference organizer, by "shattering irrelevance."[11] To be sure, many of the "private individuals" were planted to achieve various desired effects, but of the 1,800 persons who attended the meeting a large number took the invitation to free expression quite literally, and some 200 youths from both rich and poor countries promptly organized and encamped themselves in a "New Earth Village" (barracks supplied by the Dutch government). Their slogan was "Do not adjust your mind—there is a fault in reality," their tactics were bracing, and they proceeded more or less to set the tone of the conference, or at least turn it down an unexpected road. Some people, according to the secretary general of the conference, were "shocked beyond measure,"[12] while others were delighted to hear young people say what has previously been left unsaid.

On the eve of the conference, the "New Earth Village" held its own meeting and sent John Danquah, of Ghana, with "the point of youth" for the congress to hear. The rich countries, he said, were suspect in the way they maintained a constant interest in the poor, "yet ignore that same poverty, hunger, and racism at home." The FAO and the other United Nations organizations, Danquah charged, "tend to support the existing political systems," and the FAO in particular was "intimately intertwined with the vested interests of western countries." He said that an examination of all those institutions that were helping the underdeveloped countries would reveal a "monumental hypocrisy." Governments, the UN, the church, and private organizations, while claiming to fight underdevelopment, "maintain those structures which cause that self-same underdevelopment."[13]

Danquah's message was felt by many of the institution-servers to have been too "negative" and "counterproductive." The FAO director general went to the "New Earth Village," had a photograph taken of himself sitting on the ground powwowing with young people, and said that while he agreed with many of their theories, there were practical realities that had to be dealt with.

Other participants sought to "refine" the militancy of youth in the "final declaration" of the congress, but, in fact, this document added more than it subtracted, showing that there was a role for the not so young, too. It focused on the social potentials of the green revolution and rejected external pressures for population control, as well as the neo-Malthusian view in general, which had been actively advanced by the institution-servers throughout the conference.[14]

"A green revolution is underway," it said. "The total development of every man, woman, and child is at stake. It is thwarted by injustice, exploitation, discrimination and all manifestations of human selfishness." Only a radical transformation of contemporary power structures could alter this situation, said the declaration, and land reform, above all, was needed "to enhance the status and dignity of rural people, improve their incomes, and release their energies for increased production." This was a matter "too important to be left only to the experts." [15]

While this declaration was being hammered out, the London *Sunday Times* disclosed that Washington a few days earlier had warned the organization privately "that if FAO becomes too political America's contributions might be cut." [16] On the day that the declaration was published, the FAO, at the final session of the congress, reserved the right to disown any and all of its recommendations and declarations. It could not do anything it said, "that antagonized governments to the point of getting the Organization's throat cut." [17]

Everyone went home. The Organization's throat still pulses regularly. The whole Family is feeling as well as can be expected. *All* of the Organizations are more or less intact. The Old Order controls the New. The green revolution is in the hands of the Experts. A giant is in the earth.

NOTES ON SOURCES

1. See T. R. Malthus, *An Essay on the Principle of Population,* London: J. Johnson, 1798, pp. 177–208. This is the first edition of Malthus' book. The quotations from Godwin are in *ibid.* pp. 177–79, 180. They are taken from *Political Justice,* first published in 1793. The two words in brackets "[and moral]" were omitted in all six editions of Malthus' work, as were the changes Godwin made in later editions of his work.

Prologue

1. L. Mumford, *The City in History,* London: Penguin Books, 1966, p. 21; cf. Mumford, *The Myth of the Machine,* New York: Harcourt Brace, 1967.

2. G. Vico, *The New Science,* New York: Anchor Books, 1961, p. 128.

3. Muggeridge quoted in C. Clark, *Starvation or Plenty,* London: Secker and Warburg, 1970, p. 171.

Chapter I

1. N. Borlaug, "Wheat, Rust, and People," in *Phytopathology,* 55: 1965, p. 1097.

2. See E. Flores, "The Big Threat Is Not Hunger," in *Ceres,* May-June, 1969, p. 19; cf. R. Dumont and B. Rosier, *The Hungry Future,* London: Andre Deutsch, 1969, p. 18.

3. W. and P. Paddock, *Famine—1975!,* Boston: Little, Brown, 1967, pp. 212–29.

4. P. Ehrlich, *The Population Bomb,* New York: Ballantine Books, 1968, p. 11.

5. *Ibid.*

6. Borlaug quoted in the *International Herald Tribune* (*IHT*), Oct. 24–25, 1970.

7. Borlaug quoted in the *Times* of London, Nov. 13, 1970.

8. For the background on the development of the high-yielding dwarf wheats and rice, see, for example: *Indicative World Plan for Agricultural Development,* Rome: FAO, 1969, 3 vols. (hereinafter cited as *IWP*); L. Brown, *Seeds of Change,* New York: Praeger, 1970 (and Brown's bibliography); D. Paarlberg, *Norman Borlaug—Hunger Fighter,* Washington: Government Printing Office, 1970; D. Dalrymple, *Imports and Plantings of High-Yielding Varieties,* Washington: Government Printing Office, 1971; rev. ed., 1972; *Five Years of Research on Dwarf Wheats,* New Delhi, IARI, 1968; C. Streeter, *India* (a 138-page report published by the Rockefeller Foundation in 1969); *High-Yielding Varieties of Grain Food Crops,* Rome: FAO, 1969; N. Borlaug, *op. cit.;* N. Borlaug, "A Green Revolution," *Columbia Journal of World Business,* 4:1969; E. Flores, *op. cit.;* L. Brown, "The Agricultural Revolution in Asia," *Foreign Affairs,* July, 1968; C. Wharton, "The Green Revolution: Cornucopia or Pandora's Box," *Foreign Affairs,* Apr. 1969; W. Ladejinsky, "Ironies of India's Green Revolution," *Foreign Affairs,* July 1970.

9. Paarlberg, *op cit.,* p. 11.

10. Brown, *Seeds of Change,* p. 15.

11. Borlaug, "Wheat, Rust," p. 1089.

12. *Ibid.,* p. 1090.

13. *Ibid.,* p. 1088.

14. Interviews with M. S. Swaminathan, New Delhi, Apr. 9, 12, 1971 (hereinafter cited as *ints. MSS*).

15. Paarlberg, *op. cit.,* p. 15.

16. I. Narvaez and N. Borlaug, *Accelerated Wheat Improvement in West Pakistan and the Revolution in Agriculture* (unpublished ms. in FAO library).

17. Paddock, *Famine,* p. 8.

18. Reproduced in W. Barclay, J. Enright, and R. Reynolds, "Population Control in the Third World" in *NACLA Newsletter,* Dec. 1970 (hereinafter cited as *Barclay report;* see Chapter III).

19. Snow quoted in *Newsweek,* Feb. 3, 1969, p. 43.
20. Brown, "Agricultural Revolution," p. 43.
21. McNamara quoted in *Newsweek,* Feb. 3, 1969, p. 43.
22. Dalrymple, *op. cit.,* p. 43.
23. *IWP,* vol. 3, p. 26.
24. Ehrlich quoted in W. Paddock, "How Green Is the Green Revolution" in *Bio Science,* Aug. 15, 1970, p. 901.
25. *Ibid.,* p. 897.
26. Wharton, *op cit.*
27. O. Freeman, "Agriculture 2000" in *Mediterranea,* July-Sept., 1967, pp. 169–78.
28. The material for the scenario was drawn primarily from the following: Pawley, *op. cit.;* T. Gordon, "Food in the Future" in R. Farmer, *et al.* (eds.), *World Population—The View Ahead,* Bloomington, Ind.: Indiana University Press, 1968, pp. 168–84; F. Steward, "Cloning Cells and Controlling the Composition of Crops" in *Progress,* 2: 1970, pp. 44–51; A. Galston, "Crops Without Chemicals" in *New Scientist and Science Journal,* June 3, 1971, pp. 577–79; F. Simmonds, "Biological Control of Pests" in *Tropical Science,* 12:3, 1970, pp. 191–99; G. Neuray, "L'Agriculture en l'an 2000" in *Economie rurale,* Jan.-Mar. 1971, pp. 3–12; J. Howard, "New Proteins: Animal, Vegetable, Mineral" in *New Scientist and Science Journal,* Feb. 25, 1971, pp. 438–39; Clark, *op. cit.,* pp. 154–71; "Man into Superman" in *Time,* Apr. 19, 1971, pp. 21–36; J. Watson, "Moving Toward the Clonal Man" in *The Atlantic,* pp. 50–53.
29. W. Pawley, "How Can There Be Secured Food For All?" (unpublished ms.), p. 7; an abbreviated version titled "In the Year 2070" may be found in *Ceres,* July-Aug. 1971, pp. 22–27.
30. *Ibid.,* p. 4.

Chapter II

1. The literature on the population problem is immense, to say the least. Some of the published books especially relevant to this work which I found useful (apart from the standard statistical materials, monographs, and articles) include: Clark, *op. cit.;* C. Clark, *Population Growth and Land Use,* London: Macmillan, 1967; A. Sauvy, *Théorie générale de la population,* Paris, 1954, 2 vols.; E. Boserup, *The Conditions of Agricultural Growth,* London: Allen

and Unwin, 1965; J. Beshers, *Population Processes in Social Systems,* New York: The Free Press, 1967; A. Allison (ed.), *Population Control,* London: Penguin Books, 1970; L. Stamp, *Our Developing World,* London: Faber and Faber, 1968; G. Myrdal, *Asian Drama,* New York: Pantheon Books, 1968.

2. Cf. Clark, *Starvation or Plenty,* pp. 47–48.

3. Quoted in K. Abercrombie, "Changing Views on the Man-Food Relationship" in *Ceres,* Mar.-Apr. 1971, p. 22.

4. Quoted in *ibid.,* p. 23.

5. Malthus, *op. cit.,* 1817 ed., p. 512.

6. K. Boulding, *The Image,* Ann Arbor: University of Michigan Press, 1956, quoted in Paddock, "How Green," p. 902.

7. See Malthus, *op. cit.,* 1817 ed., pp. 382–82.

8. See Boserup, *op. cit.*

9. See *ibid.;* Clark, *Population Growth,* pp. 133–38; Clark, *Starvation or Plenty,* pp. 47–50; see also E. Boserup, "Population Growth and Food Supplies" in Allison, *op. cit.,* pp. 152–64; P. von Blanckenburg and M. Schulz, "The Socio-Economic Context of Agricultural Innovation Processes," in *Zeitschrift für ausländishe Landwirtschaft,* Dec. 1970, pp. 319-320.

10. Boserup, *Conditions,* pp. 62-63; cf. Clark, *Starvation or Plenty,* p. 88.

11. Boserup, *Conditions,* p. 54.

12. See, for example, J. Weeks, "Uncertainty, Risk and Wealth and Income Distribution in Peasant Agriculture" in the *Journal of Development Studies,* 7:1, 1970, pp. 28-36.

13. "Evolutionary Hopes and Fears" in the *Times Literary Supplement,* Oct. 22, 1971.

14. Ehrlich, *op. cit.,* p. 135.

15. E.g., Ehrlich's ZPG, Inc.; the newest is the Coalition for a National Population Policy, headed by Milton Eisenhower, and supported by 58 U.S. Congressmen.

16. *Population Growth and America's Future,* Washington: Government Printing Office, 1971, pp. 10-11.

17. Sauvy, *op. cit.,* vol. 2, p. 20.

18. Boserup, *Conditions;* Clark, *Population Growth,* p. 135; von Blanckenburg and Schulz, *op. cit.,* p. 319.

19. See *Barclay Report,* p. 11.

20. Clark interviewed in the *Times of India,* Apr. 25, 1971.

21. *IWP,* vol. 1, p. 98.

22. H. J. Barnett, "Population Problems—Myths and Realities," in: *Economic Development and Cultural Change,* (July, 1971).

23. X. Flores, "Runaway Mechanization" in *Ceres,* July-Aug. 1971, p. 30.

24. Von Blanckenburg and Schulz, *op. cit.,* p. 319.

25. Clark, *Population Growth,* p. 135.

26. Malthus, *op. cit.,* 1817 ed., p. 512.

27. See *Barclay Report,* p. 7.

28. See Pawley, *op. cit.*

29. L. Saunders, "Beyond Family Planning" (a speech reprinted by the Ford Foundation), p. 11.

30. Paddock, "How Green," p. 901.

31. M. Burnet, *Genes, Dreams and Realities,* London: Medical and Technical Publishing, 1971, quoted in the *Times Literary Supplement, op. cit.*

32. R. Ardrey, "Birth Control in the Wilds," in *New York Times* feature service dispatch in *IHT,* Sept. 29 and 30, 1971.

33. *Barclay Report,* p. 14; see also *Population Program Assistance,* Washington: AID, 1970, pp. 153-158.

34. See *Population Program Assistance,* pp. 153-158; also interviews given to author at AID in New Delhi, Apr.-May, 1971.

35. Saunders, *op. cit.,* p. 8.

36. J. Hooker, "Annual Review of Population Problems, Malawi, 1970," to be published in a collection of papers from the Caltech Conference (held in Dec., 1970.)

37. Saunders, *op. cit.,* p. 8.

38. J. McLin, "Population Review 1970: Belgium": Caltech Conference paper to be published as above.

39. A. Sweezy, "Summary of Leading Trends and Issues," Caltech Conference paper to be published as above.

40. *Times Literary Supplement, op. cit.*

41. For a clear exposition of the photosynthetic process, see I. Asimov, *Photosynthesis,* London: Allen and Unwin, 1968.

42. See *FAO Agricultural Paper No. 90,* Rome: FAO, 1971. This document says that in some tropical countries losses run even higher than 50 percent.

43. Pawley, *op. cit.,* p. 6; see also *FAO Basic Study No. 10,* Rome: FAO, 1963.

44. *Ibid.,* p. 7.

45. C. de Wit, "Photosynthetic Limits on Crop Yields" in A.

San Pietro, *et al.* (eds.), *Harvesting the Sun,* New York: Academic Press, 1967, pp. 315-320.

46. H. Brown in an address to the American Society of Newspaper Editors, Apr. 21, 1967.

47. Pawley, *op. cit.,* p. 16.

48. L. Angenot, "Living Space," paper given at a symposium on "men in dense packing," Amsterdam, 1966, quoted in de Wit, *op. cit.,* p. 318.

49. See Clark, *Starvation or Plenty,* pp. 16-27,

50. See P. Payne and E. Wheeler, "What Protein Gap?" in *New Scientist and Science Journal,* Apr. 15, 1971, pp. 148-150.

51. See P. Ehrlich, "Famine 1975: Fact or Fallacy" in H. Helfrich (ed.), *The Environmental Crisis,* New Haven: Yale University Press, 1970, pp. 50-51.

52. Associated Press dispatch in *IHT,* July 24, 1971.

53. See especially S. Richardson, "The Influence of Social-Environmental and Nutritional Factors on Mental Ability" in N. Scrimshaw and J. Gordon (eds.), *Malnutrition, Learning, and Behavior,* Cambridge: MIT Press, 1968, pp. 346-361.

54. "Report on the 1970 Symposium of the Group of European Nutritionists" (May 1970), unpublished FAO doc. NU6/1, p. 2.

55. R. Rajalakshmi, "Short Comment" in Scrimshaw and Gordon, *op. cit.,* pp. 361-362.

56. *Ibid.,* p. 361.

57. See *Nature,* Dec. 5, 1970, p. 228.

58. K. Barrons, "Environmental Benefits of Intensive Crop Production" in *Agricultural Science Review,* Apr.-June 1971, pp. 33-39.

59. A. Toffler, *Future Shock,* London: Bodley Head, 1970, p. 27.

60. *The State of Food and Agriculture,* 1970, Rome: FAO, 1970 p. 129. (hereinafter cited as *SOFA.*)

61. *SOFA,* 1971, p. 75.

62. *SOFA,* 1971, pp. 1-2.

63. See *Agricultural Commodity Projections,* 1970-1980, Rome: FAO, 1971, vol. I.

64. Pawley, *op. cit.,* p. 8.

65. See Dumont and Rosier, *op. cit.,* p. 18

66. *Ibid.*

67. Pawley, *op. cit.,* p. 19.

Chapter III

1. For this viewpoint, see P. Ehrlich and J. Holdren, "Impact of Population Growth" in *Science,* Mar. 26, 1971, pp. 1212-1217; for an opposing view see A. Coale, "Man and His Environment" in *Science,* Oct. 9, 1970, pp. 132-136, and B. Commoner, in *Saturday Review,* 53:50, 1970.

2. See J. Ridgeway, *The Politics of Ecology,* New York: Dutton, 1970, p. 171.

3. Coale, *op. cit.,* p. 135.

4. Simmonds, *op cit.,* p. 199; see also Galston, *op cit.,* and F. Wilson, "International Boost for Biological Pest Control" in *New Scientist and Science Journal,* May 27, 1971, pp. 523-524.

5. T. Gordon, *op. cit.,* p. 180.

6. Ridgeway, *op. cit.,* p. 191.

7. K. Boulding, "Fun and Games with the Gross National Product" in Helfrich, *op. cit.,* p. 166.

8. *Ibid.,* p. 169.

9. Ehrlich, "Famine 1975," p. 63.

10. *Ibid.,* p. 55.

11. *Ibid.,* p. 59.

12. *Ibid.,* p. 48.

13. Boulding, *"Fun and Games,"* p. 170.

14. *Ibid.,* p. 168.

15. *Barclay Report,* p. 5; Ehrlich says it is 30 percent; others vary between the high and the low figures.

16. See the diagram in the *Barclay Report,* p. 6.

17. J. Rockefeller, "Why I Believe in Philanthropy" in *The Reader's Digest,* Dec. 1969, p. 190.

18. *Barclay report,* p. 4.

19. O. Harkavy, *et al.,* "Ford Foundation Strategy for Population Work" (Ford Foundation reprint adapted from *Demography,* 5:2, 1968), p. 7.

20. Ford Foundation, *Annual Report,* 1970, p. 76.

21. *Barclay Report,* p. 7.

22. See *ibid.,* pp. 5-7.

23. *Barclay report,* p. 5.

24. J. Ridgeway in *Hard Times,* June 23-30, 1969; see also Ridgeway, *Politics,* p. 194.

25. Ridgeway, *Politics,* pp. 14-15.

26. *Ibid.*, pp. 16-17.

27. See, for example, D. Gates, "Weather Modification in the Service of Mankind" in Helfrich, *op. cit.*, pp. 33-46.

28. Coale, *op. cit.*, p. 136.

29. *Nature,* Mar. 10, 1972, pp. 47-49.

30. See *New Scientist,* May 18, 1972, p. 398.

31. D. Meadows, *et al., The Limits to Growth,* New York: Universe Books, 1972, p. 23.

32. *Ibid.*, p. 194.

33. See his *World Dynamics,* Cambridge: Wright Allen Press, 1971.

34. Meadows, *op. cit.*, p. 194.

35. *Nature, op. cit.;* see also C. Kaysen, "The Computer that Printed Out WOLF," in *Foreign Affairs,* July 1972. Kaysen argues that the finiteness of earth is an irrelevancy, since it does not set limites on technology.

36. Handler quoted in *Paris Match,* May 20, 1971.

37. Statement of Feb. 2, 1971, quoted in N. Borlaug "Mankind and Civilization at Another Crossroad" (1971 McDougall Memorial Lecture), FAO DOC: C 71/LIM/4 (hereinafter referred to as *Borlaug lect.*), p. 57.

38. Quoted in the *Financial Times* (London), p. 9.

39. See *Ibid.*

40. See *Ibid.*

41. See L. Ling, *et al.*, "Persistent Insecticides in Relation to the Environment and Their Unintended Effects," Rome, 1972 (FAO DOC. AGPP:MISC/4), p. 28.

42. R. Carson, *Silent Spring,* London: Penguin Books, 1965, pp. 26-27.

43. H. Landsberg, "Population Growth and the Potential of Technology" in Farmer, *op. cit.*, p. 162.

44. *Ibid.*

45. *Ibid.*

46. Gates, *op. cit.*, p. 38.

47. See *New York Times* dispatch in *IHT,* Sept. 8, 1971; also M. Williams, "Lead Pollution on Trial" in *New Scientist and Science Journal,* Sept. 9, 1971, pp. 578-80.

48. F. Ross, "Sulphur Dioxide Over Britain and Beyond" in *New Scientist and Science Journal,* May 13, 1971, pp. 373-376.

49. M. Fontaine, "Marine Pollution: Can We Control it to Advantage?" in *Ceres,* May-June, 1969, pp. 32-35.

50. See *Ceres,* May-June, 1971, p. 9.
51. Landsberg, *op. cit.*, p. 141.
52. Coale, *op. cit.*, p. 133.
53. *Ibid.*
54. Landsberg, *op. cit.*, p. 160 (his emphasis).
55. *Ibid.*, p. 158.
56. *Los Angeles Times* dispatch in *IHT*, Sept. 8, 1971.
57. Landsberg, *op. cit.*, p. 141.
58. United Press International dispatch in *IHT*, Apr. 29, 1971.
59. Speech of Sept. 21, 1970 (World Bank reprint), pp. 17-23.

Chapter IV

1. G. Chedd, "Hidden Peril of the Green Revolution" in *New Scientist,* Oct. 22, 1970, pp. 171-173

2. See *Ibid.*

3. Paddock, "How Green," p. 899.

4. See, for example, P. Ehrlich, "Ecology and the War on Hunger" in *War on Hunger,* Dec. 1970, p. 2.

5. *Ibid.*

6. Interview with Khem Singh Gill, head of plant breeding department, Punjab Agricultural University, Ludhiana, Apr. 11, 1971; also K. Gill and S. Anand, "The Punjab Wheats" in *Progressive Farming,* Oct. 1970, pp. 2-6.

7. See M. Swaminathan, "Recent Research at the Indian Agricultural Research Institute" (unpublished), 1971; also *ints. MSS.*

8. *Ints. MSS.*

9. See Chedd, *op. cit.;* also various issues of *Plant Introduction Newsletter,* and FAO periodical devoted to the subject.

10. Cole quoted in Ehrlich, *Population Bomb,* p. 48.

11. *Ibid.*

12. *The Economist,* May 15, 1971, p. 39.

13. See C. Clark, *The Economics of Irrigation,* Oxford: Pergamon Press, 1970.

14. L. Brown, "Human Food Production as a Process in the Biosphere" in *Scientific American,* Sept. 1970, p. 166.

15. *Ibid.*

16. ECAFE press release no. G/52/71.

17. See A. Slack, *Defense Against Famine,* New York: Doubleday, 1970.

18. See *ibid.;* also *IWP,* and *Fertilizers and High-Yielding Varities,* Rome: FAO, 1970.

19. On fertilizer component reserves, see Slack, *op. cit.*

20. For the documentation of this argument, see R. A. Olsen, "Effects of Intensive Fertilizer Use on the Human Environment," Rome, 1972 (FAO Dec. AGL: FHE/72/10)—an extensive survey of the subject, and the summary and conclusions of an "Expert Panel" convened in Jan. 1972 for this purpose.

21. *Ibid.*

22. *Ibid.*

23. See the reports of the FAO-WHO Codez Alimentarius Commission and particularly Ling, *op. cit.*, and WHO *Technical Report Series No. 458,* 1970.

24. Ling, *op. cit.,* p. 28.

25. *Ibid.,* p. 33.

26. Borlaug writing for the North American Newspaper Alliance (NANA) dispatch of June 8, 1971.

27. *Borlaug lect.,* p. 46.

28. *Ibid.,* p. 36.

29. *Ibid.,* p. 58.

30. Cited in *Ibid.*

31. "New Scientist," May 18, 1972, p. 363.

32. See P. Boffy, "Herbicides in Vietnam," in *Science,* Aug. 1, 1971, pp. 43, 47.

33. The monographic literature on the rural exodus and Third World unemployment is vast. For a recent overview, see *Ceres,* Nov.-Dec. 1970, a special issue on the subject, particularly articles by E. Thorbecke, A. Meister, G. Hagmüller, and E. Jacoby; see also *Partners in Development,* New York: Praeger, 1969 (hereinafter cited as *Pearson Report*); Myrdal, *op. cit.*

34. J. Dyckman, quoted in Hagmüller, *op. cit.,* p. 47; cf. Jacoby, *op. cit.*

35. See, for example, Brown, *Seeds,* pp. 103-109; B. Sen, "Size of Farms and Employment of Farm Labor (unpublished, Rockefeller Foundation), 1971; also documentation for Chapter V, below.

36. S. Barraclough, "Why Land Reform?" in *Ceres,* Nov.-Dec. 1969, p. 22; see also S. Barraclough, "Institutional Coverage and Strategies for Integrated Rural Development" (unpublished paper given at an international symposium on rural development, Rome, June 1971); E. Jacoby, *Man and Land,* London: Andre

Deutsch, 1971; E. Feder, *The Rape of the Peasantry,* New York: Anchor Books, 1971.

37. His emphasis.

38. For an empirical study of this mechanism in Latin America see A. Pearse, "Structural Problems of Education Systems in Latin America" (unpublished document of the United Nations Research Institute for Social Development, no. 71/C.3).

39. M. Brown, "Don't Blame the Campesino" in *Ceres,* Sept.-Oct., 1871, pp. 29-33; see also E. Rogers, *Modernization Among Peasant,* New York: Holt, Rinehart and Winston, 1969.

Chapter V

1. See C. and Z. Loomis (eds.), *Socio-Economic Change and the Religious Factor in India,* New Delhi: Affiliated East-West Press, 1969 ("an Indian symposium of views on Max Weber").

2. See Dalrymple, *op. cit.,* pp. 9-20.

3. Quoted in L. Brown, *Seeds,* p. 6.

4. Quoted in H. Singh, "Green Revolution: Agro-Economic Analysis" in *Economic Affairs* (Calcutta), 15:10, 1970, p. 473.

5. *Ibid.*

6. *Ibid.*

7. *Ints. MSS.*

8. A. Thapar, "Seeds of Progress" in the *Times of India,* Dec. 28, 1970.

9. W. Ladejinsky, "The Green Revolution in Punjab" in *Economic and Political Weekly,* June 28, 1969.

10. Interview with Ashok Thapar, New Delhi, Apr. 16, 1971 (*int. AT*).

11. Ladejinsky, "Punjab."

12. Ladejinsky, "Ironies," p. 768.

13. "The Causes and Nature of Current Agrarian Tensions," New Delhi, 1969.

14. P. Kellner, "Bitter Harvest from the Green Revolution" in the *Sunday Times* (London), June 28, 1970.

15. See "The Causes and Nature."

16. Ladejinsky, "Ironies," p. 766.

17. *Ibid.,* p. 767.

18. *Times of India,* Sept. 8, 1970.

19. I. Singh and C. Gilpatric, "Advance and Problems in New High-Yielding Varieties" (unpublished paper given at a symposium

on wheat research, Uttar Pradesh Agricultural University, Pantnagar, Mar. 15, 1971); see also UPAU, *Changing Agriculture and Rural Life,* Pantnagar: 1967-68, 2 vols.; UPAU, *Changing Agriculture in Two Regions of Uttar Pradesh in 1969-70,* Pantnagar, 1971; also interview with C. Gilpatric, New Delhi, Apr. 8, 1971 (*int. CG*).

20. W. Hendrix, "The Green Revolution in India," New Delhi: AID (unpublished), 1970; also *int. CG,* and interview with W. Hendrix, New Delhi, Apr. 14, 1971 (*int. WH*), interview with R. Olsen, New Delhi, Apr. 14, 1971 (*int. RS*).

21. See especially T. Oommen, "Green Revolution and Agrarian Conflict in India" (unpublished), 1970; T. Oommen, "The Politics of Land Grab Agitation" (unpublished), 1970; T. Oommen, "Non-Violent Approach to Land Reform" in *Zeitschrift für ausländische Landwirtschaft,* Mar. 1970, pp. 44-55; A. Beteille, "Harmonic and Disharmonic Systems" in *Seminar,* Apr. 1971, pp. 16-19; G. Parthasarathy, "Rural Power Structure" in *Seminar,* Apr. 1971, pp. 23-25; cf. the bibliography in *Seminar,* Apr. 1971, pp. 44-47; also interview with T. Oommen, New Delhi, Apr. 20, 1971 (*int. TO*).

22. B. Nussbaum, in *Far Eastern Economic Review,* Oct. 31, 1970, p. 30.

23. *Int. AT.*

24. T. Drieberg, "India's Agro-Industry is Trying to Catch Up" in *Ceres,* Mar.-Apr. 1971, p. 60; also interview with T. Drieberg, New Delhi, Apr. 12, 1971 (*int. TD*).

25. See the published series of "scheme" literature of the Indian Ministry of Food and Agriculture, Mar. 1971.

26. C. Subramaniam, "The Case of the Seventies" in *Seminar,* Apr. 1971, p. 15.

27. *Ibid.,* p. 13.

28. *Int. TO.*

29. Drieberg, *op. cit.,* p. 62.

30. Interview with B. Venkatappiah, New Delhi, Apr. 14, 1971.

31. See A. Meister, "The Yugoslav Experiment" in *Ceres,* Mar.-Apr. 1971, pp. 39-41; also Jacoby, *op. cit.,* for other examples.

32. See von Blanckenburg and Schulz, *op. cit.,* p. 319.

33. A. Thapar, "Helping Small Farmers" in the *Times of India,* Apr. 15, 1971.

34. Singh and Gilpatric, *op. cit.;* see also Hendrix, *op. cit.*

35. *New York Times* dispatch in *IHT,* Sept. 20, 1971.

36. *ints. MSS; int. AT.*

37. Swaminathan, "Recent Research"; see also M. Swaminathar *et al.,* "Scientific Multiple Cropping" in *World Science News,* 7:7, pp. 9-22; "Green Revolution—the Next Phase," a special issue of *World Science News,* 8:3, with articles by Borlaug, Swaminathan, J. Hutchinson, *et al.*

Chapter VI

1. See rev. ed. of Dalrymple, *op. cit.,* issued in Feb. 1972 as *Foreign Economic Development Report—14.*

2. *IWP.*

3. E. Venezian and W. Gamble, *The Agricultural Development of Mexico,* New York: Praeger, 1969, quoted in R. Stavenhagen, "Mexico's Past Growth" in *Ceres,* July-Aug. 1970, p. 53.

4. Venezian and Gamble, *op. cit.,* quoted in Stavenhagen, *op. cit.,* p. 55.

5. cf. Stavenhagen, *op. cit.,* p. 55; see also I. Navarrette, "The Cost of a Job," in *Ceres,* Sept.-Oct. 1971, pp. 53-57.

6. *The Economist,* Mar. 27, 1971, p. 83.

7. A. Gaitskill, "Problems of Land Reform in Southeast Asia" (unpublished paper given at a seminar, University of London, May 8, 1968).

8. Jacoby, *op. cit.,* pp. 360-371.

9. See *Newsweek,* Feb. 3, 1969, pp. 43-44.

10. See C. Snyder, "Marx Versus Malthus" in *Far Eastern Economic Review,* Dec. 26, 1970, pp. 28-32.

11. H. Löwenstein, "A Crowded Journey" in *Ceres,* Mar.-Apr. 1971, p. 51.

12. Snyder, *op. cit.,* p. 31.

13. FAO Pree Release no. 72/49 Co 4.

14. Dalrymple, *op. cit.,* p. 40.

15. *SOFA,* 1971, p. 89.

16. *SOFA,* 1970, p. 96.

17. "The Rice Situation in China (Mainland)" (FAO Doc. no. CCP:RI 71/C.R.S./3)

18. FAO Press Release no 72/49 Co 4.

19. Dalrymple, *op. cit.,* p. 41.

20. *Sunday Times* (London), Feb. 15, 1970.
21. United Press International dispatch in *IHT*, Aug. 7, 1971.
22. Rev. ed. of Dalrymple, *op. cit.*, p. 55.
23. Quoted in *ibid.*
24. Quoted in *ibid.*
25. *Ibid.*
26. Quoted in *ibid.* p. 56.
27. *Ibid.*
28. *Ibid.*
29. See Yudelman, *op. cit.*, p. 27.
30. *IWP*, vol. 1, p. 103.
31. Yudleman, *op. cit.*, p. 18.
32. X. Flores, *op. cit.*, p. 28.
33. *SOFA*, 1971, p. 82.
34. Yudelman, *op. cit.*, p. 18.
35. *Ibid.*
36. FAO Press Release no. 72/51-Co 5.
37. *Ibid.*, p. 27.
38. "Southeast Asia's Economy in the 1970s" quoted in ADB press release no. 52/70; cf. A. Boerma, "ACC Functional Group on the Green Revolution" (FAO document DDL: 71/3 (rev.), p. 16 (hereinafter cited as *Boerma paper*).
39. *Boerma paper*, p. 15.
40. *Far East Trade and Development*, quoted in *Ceres*, Mar.-Apr. 1971, p. 21.
41. N. Cervantes in the *Manila Chronicle*, quoted in *Ceres*, Nov.-Dec. 1970, p. 19.
42. L. Goodstadt, in *Far Eastern Economic Review*, Feb. 27, 1971, p. 19.
43. See Yudelman, *op. cit.*, p. 18; and *Boerma paper*.
44. Yudelman, *op. cit.*, p. 18 (his emphasis).
45. See *Times of India*, Mar. 17 and April 17, 1972, especially the columns of Ashok Thapar.
46. E. Flores, *op. cit.*, p. 21; see also *Boerma paper*, and FAO press release no. 70/169/CO/38, of Nov. 3, 1970 ("Green Revolution May Upset Trade Patterns, FAO Commodity Group Warns").

Chapter VII

1. Figures from *Pearson report.*

2. Interview with G. Myrdal in *Ceres,* Mar.-Apr. 1971, p. 34.

3. *Effective Aid,* Washington: Overseas Development Institute, 1966, p. 34.

4. M. de Silva, in *Far Eastern Economic Review,* quoted in *Ceres,* Sept.-Oct. 1970, p. 15.

5. *World Bank Report,* quoted in T. Rought, "The World Bank: Five-Year Plan" in *Far Eastern Economic Review,* Apr. 3, 1971, p. 80; see also *New York Times,* Sept. 24, 1970, p. 6.

6. Interview with J. Nyerere, in *The Internationalist,* Oct. 1970, p. 6; see also J. Nyerere, *Freedom and Unity,* Dar es Salaam: Oxford University Press, 1966.

7. R. Heilbroner, "The Multinational Corporation and the Nation State" in the *New York Review of Books,* Feb. 11, 1971, p. 22.

8. G. Ranis and J. Nelson, "Measures to Ensure the Effective Use of Aid," *AID Discussion Paper No. 9,* p. 91.

9. Heilbroner, *op. cit.,* p. 23.

10. See I. Horowitz (ed.), *The Rise and Fall of Project Camelot,* Cambridge: MIT Press, 1967.

11. See E. Wolf and J. Jorgenson, "Anthropology on the Warpath in Thailand" in the *New York Review of Books,* Nov. 19, 1970, pp. 26-34.

12. See the report of the Africa Research Group: *The Extended Family,* 1970.

13. J. Hanlon, "The Implications of Project Cambridge" in *New Scientist and Science Journal,* Feb. 25, 1971, p. 422.

14. Nicolaus quoted in E. Wolf and J. Jorgenson, *op. cit.,* p. 29.

15. Yntema quoted in Hanlon, *op. cit.,* p. 422.

16. World Bank, *Annual Report,* 1966-67, p. 6.

17. *Foreign Agriculture,* May 31, 1971, p. 6.

18. On Ball see Heilbroner, *op. cit.,* p. 21; on Jacoby, N. Jacoby, "The Multinational Corporation" in *The Center Magazine,* May 1970, pp. 37-55; on the multinationals in general, see L. Turner, *Invisible Empires,* New York: Harcourt, 1971, and C. Kindleberger (ed.), *The International Corporation,* Cambridge: MIT Press, 1970.

19. T. Hayter, *Aid as Imperialism,* London: Penguin Books, 1971, pp. 151-152

20. *Ibid.*, p. 159.
21. World Bank, *Annual Report,* 1970.
22. *Sunday Times* (London), June 28, 1970.
23. Interview with D. Tweddle in *Ceres,* Sept.-Oct., 1970, p. 23.
24. E. Jacoby, *Man and Land,* p. 141.
25. Interview with Tweddle, *op. cit.*, p. 27.
26. X. Lamy, "Overcoming Suspicion" in *Ceres,* Sept.-Oct. 1969, p. 44; see also E. Jacoby, *Man and Land,* pp. 144-147.
27. Quoted in Lamy, *op. cit.*, p. 43.
28. E. Jacoby, *Man and Land,* p. 147.
29. *Boerma paper;* see also FAO document no. DDL/70/3, 1970.
30. ECO SOC Doc. no. E/5012, Part II.
31. *Ibid.*, p. 14.
32. *Ibid.*, p. 17.
33. *Ibid.*, p. 11.
34. *Ibid.*, p. 8.
35. *Ibid.*
36. See *Land Reform: Annotated Bibliography,* Rome: FAO, 1971.
37. *Boerma paper,* p. 4.
38. *Ibid.*, pp. 12-13.

Chapter VIII

1. Speech of Sept. 21, 1970, in *op. cit.*, p. 18.
2. *Ibid.*, p. 21.
3. *Ibid.*, p. 19.
4. *Ibid.*
5. *Ibid.*, pp. 21-23.
6. Jacoby, *op. cit.*, p. 54.
7. N. Jacoby, "The Progress of Peoples: Toward a Theory and Policy of Development with External Aid" in *A Center Occasional Paper,* 2:4, 1969, p. 22.
8. Goulet in *Ibid.*, p. 25.
9. T. Lynn Smith, "The Dead Weight of Latifundism" in *Ceres,* Sept.-Oct. 1971, pp. 59-65.
10. *Ibid.;* see also F. Cardoso, *Sociologie du développement en Amérique Latine,* Paris: Editions Anthropos, 1969, and J. de

Castro, *Géopolitique de la faim,* Paris: Editions Economie et Humanisme, 1971 (rev. ed.).

11. Tweddle in *op. cit.,* p. 23.

12. *Ibid.,* p. 26.

13. Text of Donquan's speech, in *Report of the Second World Food Congress,* Rome, FAO, 1970, vol. 1 pp. 101-105.

14. See especially the intervention of Josué de Castro; cf. J. de Castro, *op. cit.*

15. Text of final declaration in *Report of the Second World Food Congress,* vol. 1, p. 63.

16. *Sunday Times* (London), June 28, 1970.

17. See *Report of the Second World Food Congress,* vol. 1, pp. 123-130.

ACKNOWLEDGMENTS

I WOULD LIKE TO THANK the many people who in one way or another contributed to the realization of this book. I am particularly grateful to those who gave generously of their time for both interviews and discussion, often quite lengthy. I have quoted from some of them in this book, but many others were no less important in contributing to my understanding of this subject. It would not be possible, nor in every case prudent, to mention everyone, and some, they have told me, would prefer to remain anonymous.

In any event, I alone am wholly responsible for the presentation and accuracy of the material on these pages and for its interpretation.

I wish to express my appreciation to the following persons: Annika Bornstein, Birgitta Cosmatos, Yorga Pan Cosmatos, Trevor Drieberg, John Funari, Khem Singh Gill, Chadbourne Gilpatric, P. Hanumappa, Jagjit Sing Hara, Beverly Katz, K. C. Naik, K. K. Nair, Russell Olsen, Peter Matson, T. K. Oommen, Mahinderpal Singh, M. S. Swaminathan, and Ashok Thapar.

A special note of thanks to Beth and Probhat Roy; and to András Biró, the chief editor and guiding hand of *Ceres*, a most praiseworthy publication, which offers a running critique on economic and social development in the underdeveloped world.

Finally, I am thankful for the services rendered to me by the following institutions: Andra Pradesh Agricultural University, the Ford Foundation, the Indian Agricultural Research Institute, the Library of Food and Agriculture Organization of the United Nations, the Ministry of Food and Agriculture of India, the National Commission on Agriculture of India, the National Commission on Planning of India, the New York Public Library, Punjab Agricultural University, the Rockefeller Foundation, the United States Agency for International Development, and the University of Agricultural Sciences at Hebbal, Bangalore.

INDEX

Index

Index

Index

Index

Index

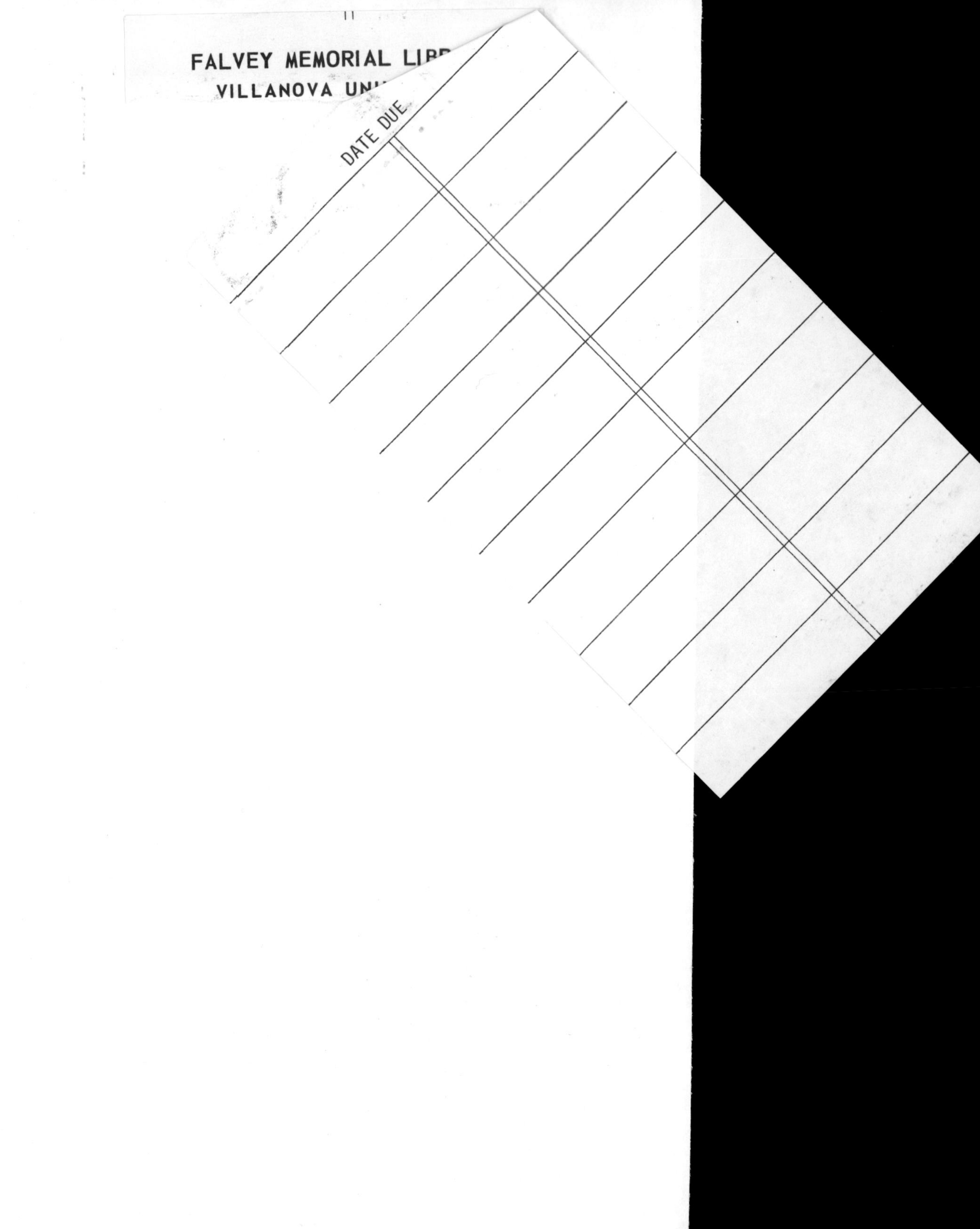
FALVEY MEMORIAL LIBR
VILLANOVA UNI
DATE DUE